305.4 Rayner, William P.
RAY
    Wise women

Date

DATE

WISE
WOMEN

SINGULAR
LIVES
THAT HELPED
SHAPE
OUR CENTURY

WISE
WOMEN

WILLIAM P. RAYNER

Foreword by

FRANCINE DU PLESSIX GRAY

Design by

MIKI DENHOF

St. Martin's Press
New York

Library of Congress Cataloging in Publication Data

Rayner, William P.
  Wise women.

    1. Women——United States——Interviews.   I. Title.
HQ1412.R38   1983   305.4'0973   83-9589
ISBN 0-312-88415-X

First Edition

10 9 8 7 6 5 4 3 2 1

To the wisest
of them all
C.H.R.
&
B.B.P.

CONTENTS

vii

ACKNOWLEDGMENTS

My thanks first go to Diana Edkins who helped me in incalculable ways on the research of this book both for locating the photographs and obtaining the background information on those to be interviewed. To Miki Denhof I owe a great debt for the time and effort she gave in designing the book. Without them it would never have come into existence.

I would be less than candid if I did not reveal that Linda Hackett and Bill Cunningham spent endless hours and exercised their considerable talents tracking down some of the more diffident of my wise women in order to photograph them in their natural habitat. To them I am truly grateful.

This project could not have been begun had it not been for the help of Dr. Lee Hall, the President of the Rhode Island School of Design; Dr. Jackie Mattfield, Vice President of Academic Affairs, The College of Charleston; Lady Nancy Keith; Melva Weber, a Health Editor of *Vogue* magazine; Betty Sherrill of McMillen, Inc.; Beverly Brannon, curator of the Frissell Collection, Library of Congress; and Marietta Tree, former Ambassador to the United Nations. Their help in suggesting distinguished women I might interview was basic to the whole project.

My special gratitude goes to Jeff Weiss and Jean Read, whose idea this book was, as well as to the eagle-eyed editors at St. Martin's Press, Tom Dunne, Ashton Applewhite, Pamela Dorman, and Deborah Daly.

I would also like to thank Robyn Douglas and Pat Sattler, both of whom were invaluable help in completing the book.

Finally, I want to thank my wife who never complained when I refused to go out for dinner, so that I could stay home with twenty-one wise women.

FOREWORD

Among the many misogynic attitudes that delayed the emancipation of women, two central notions prevail. One is the clear prejudice that views women as creatures intellectually inferior to men, as a perniciously sensual, primitive force that tends to undermine moral values and the progress of rational thought. Another form, a radically opposite and subtler one, idealizes women as the purer, more spiritual gender, as the guardians of ethical standards whose function is to civilize man's cruder, more primal energies.

The first, dismal view, particularly prevalent in Teutonic cultures, continues the condemnation implicit in the myth of Eve in the Garden: Woman as the bestial, retrogressive force, Tempted and Temptress responsible for our sins, vessel of humanity's irrational drives. This persuasion informs Nietzsche's definition of woman as "more barbarous than man"; George Meredith's conclusion that she is "The last thing civilized by man"; and Freud's statement that "Women represent the interest of family and sexual life," retarding "the work of civilization" carried forward by men. This style of disparagement makes us clearly unfit to rule in courts of law, handle microscopes, wield surgical knives or—God forbid—take on the burden of governing cities, counties, and nations.

The subtler type of misogyny, abundant in Latin and Roman Catholic cultures, views woman as creatures of such moral delicacy and spiritual refinement that they would do a disservice to society by tainting themselves with its more arduous business. However imbued with Henry Adams' belief that we have "preserved the customs of civility, supplied the intelligence, and dictated the taste," this bias dictates that we accomplish those functions within the confines of the home and the immediate community. It is this attitude that has led men to place us on pedestals in order to keep us in place, glossing us with such flattering attributes as diligence, modesty, and a capacity for nurturing regarded as uniquely ours. It is within the confines of this prejudice that we have been the only segment of humanity idealized into powerlessness. Misogyny II doesn't shout "You're not (good) (intelligent) (industrious) enough to be a lawyer." It pleads "You're too fragile and precious to survive out there; you'll get (mugged) (raped) on the way to the subway; *don't forget you have a home.*"

It is inevitable that both styles of disparagement should coexist in the ethnic melting pot of the American psyche, equally perilous to women because they deal with stereotypes, fears, and mythologies, rather than realities. This volume of William Rayner's delineates the careers of twenty-one extraordinary American women who, in pursuing their vocations, have had to confront a full share of both prejudices. It deals, in essence, with the victory of character over prejudice, the triumph of individual volition over collective myth. If there is one fundamental premise behind the writing of this book, it is the author's belief that "for generations we have been wasting one half of the creative potential of humanity by ignoring women's intellect." And he has documented his credo by choosing women in a vast variety of professions—from banking to Gestalt psychology, from publishing to social anthropology and consumer advocacy—whose dedication, idealism, and sheet gumption overcame the biases that stood in their paths.

One quotation in particular stood out in my mind as I finished reading these profiles: Mary Ingraham Bunting's conclusion that society's failure to offer equal opportunities to women "suggests something sinister—a deep fear of the results."

The subtitle of Mr. Rayner's book might well have been "Profiles in Courage." The obstacles some of these women faced in entering vocations previously reserved for men were formidable. And it is a courage that has nothing to do with passive fortitude —the ladylike valor taught us for centuries—but with a pioneering, almost militant outspokenness. *Constance Baker Motley,* the first black woman in our history to be appointed to a Federal Judgeship, the first to argue a case before our Supreme Court, grew up in a culture of poverty that forbade her any form of education beyond high school. It was her glaring candor at a meeting of a Black Community Center in her native Connecticut —at which she harshly criticized the white man who had endowed the center for not having any blacks on his board—that enabled her to fulfill her talents. The very philantrophist under attack was so impressed with her statement that he went on to finance her education through six years of college and law school. His foresight had extraordinary results. Motley went on to argue eleven cases before the Supreme Court, winning nine of them. One of them was the historic *Brown vs. Topeka, Kansas School Board,* which ruled in favor of desegregating all public schools in the United States.

There are other examples of courage in these pages less confrontational, more domestic, and as noble as Judge Motley's. *Mary Bunting*'s rise in the academic profession was perhaps delayed, but never arrested, by the fact that she was left widowed in her thirties, with four children to support. *Clarabelle Williams,* a Texas school teacher, the first black to be graduated from New Mexico State College, exemplifies that Penelopean fortitude that has to do with profound love. She and her husband-to-be remained engaged for ten years because of their respective decisions to finance the education of their younger siblings. The three sons born from this patiently-awaited union are themselves something of an American phenomenon. All of them had earned their medical degrees by the 1950s, at a time when blackness was as great an obstacle as femaleness in the pursuit of a medical vocation. They are still running a clinic together in the Woodlawn section of Chicago in which their mother worked full time for decades after her retirement from teaching—in fact, until the age of ninety.

Interwoven with the themes of courage, idealism, and persistence is a subtext to Mr. Rayner's book, which concerns a problem much debated these days in any discussion of women's roles. To what degree can women manage, simultaneously and harmoniously, a family and a career? The sensitivity of this issue was painfully evidenced by the outcry over Betty Friedan's last book, *The Second Stage,* in which she reemphasized the values of family life and the emotional needs of women in their childbearing years. Any citizen who took a stand in this controversy will be interested in the ways the women documented in *Wise Women* have balanced the demands of home and vocation.

Rosalyn Yalow, winner of the Nobel Prize for the Physiology of Medicine, waited nine years after marriage, until her career was well established, before starting a family. She is said to have come home every day at lunch time during her children's school years, to make sure that the family's religious traditions were observed, and that her children maintained a proper Kosher diet.

The artist *Aline Porter,* however, seems to be totally serene with the reverse choice—taking ten years from her career to raise three sons.

Esther Peterson, who since her twenties has been an activist in the Unionist, Feminist, Civil Rights, and Consumers' Movements, raised four children. Each of them, at various times, was brought by their mother to Capitol Hill during the decade in which she was working as lobbyist for the Amalgamated Clothing Workers' Union. "I could, if necessary, park them in Senator Estes Kefauver's office."

The motto of Esther Peterson's life, according to the author, is "Love is Wanting the Other Person to Grow." None of these profiles better exemplify that sentiment than the life of *Millicent McIntosh,* the admirable former President of Barnard College. She gave birth to five children in the alarming span of six years during her previous post as headmistress of the Brearley School. She attributes this accomplishment to her husband, a prominent professor of pediatrics whom she describes as "secure enough in his own self-esteem to put his wife's career ahead of his own." A passionate and persistent supporter of his wife's vocation, Dr. McIntosh is a man who believes that "the worst mother is the twenty-four hour mother," that "effective motherhood is not dependent on the *amount* of time that the mother spends with her child, but on the *quality* of time you give your children."

Throughout this brief foreword I have studiously avoided the term "role model," which along with "lifestyle" has been so abused, that both should be reserved as names for cats or pet rabbits. I would rather describe our situation—the one presented in Mr. Rayner's book—as the Odysseizing of Women, the Penelopizing of Men. We are facing an interesting and difficult future in which many of us will be offered a legal, medical, academic, or business position in Chicago while the man we love prefers to retain his practice in New York; in which many women will be working on the night shift at the hospital, or pleading a case in court at ten P.M., when there is a family of children at home to be fed, civilized, and put to bed. Can the millions of single parents in the United States take on the double task of Odysseus and Penelope? Can men be Penelopized enough to share fully in tasks of nurturing, assigned for millenia to women alone? The careers of the women profiled in this volume point to the possibility that with a sizeable measure of self-discipline and sacrifice these roles can be combined. As Mary Ingraham Bunting remarks (attributing the truism to Louis Pasteur), "Chance favors the prepared mind."

But the first task of any movement of emancipation is to demythologize. The women in these pages, for the most part, have been loners. A massive record of equal achievements will only be possible within a society that has purged itself of all stereotyping of gender; that has come to accept that some women are more rational, self-reliant, skilled at mechanics, hunting, and mathematics than their men; and that some men are more dependent, more instinctual, more gifted at the art of nurturing, and more talkative on the telephone than their women—a society, in sum, that accepts the reality of life.

Francine du Plessix Gray
March 1983

INTRODUCTION

When in a candid mood, I am forced to admit that women have been a much greater influence in my life than men. Whatever understanding of literature I have, I owe to my mother, who read poetry to me at an early age; whatever understanding of art, I owe to an aunt who took me to galleries and museums from the time I could balance on two legs; and whatever understanding of decency and beauty I have, I owe to my wife, who undertook the monumental responsibility of trying to civilize me many years ago. I have been blessed in having these three wise women in my life.

In actual fact there was a fourth who gave me the idea for this book. She was my wife's grandmother. Granny was a venerable ninety-year-old woman who had seen much of this world and remembered it all. As the granddaughter of a pioneer who had settled in what now is Toledo, Ohio, she remembered the Victorian house in which she was born, fronted by its large veranda with the swinging chair and hanging wisteria. She remembered the clop-clop of the horses' hooves and the grinding of the surrey's wheels out front beyond the picket fence. She recalled President William McKinley's visit and her introduction to him. She remembered her father's logging camp up on the northern peninsula of Michigan and her summers there with her sisters and cousins in the big cabin, canoeing on the Grayling River and playing with her pet doe down in the meadow. That, grinning, she would claim, was "how the Midwest was won."

I thought to tape our conversations, if only to preserve an account of the way of life in a tiny piece of this country before it got lost in the tidal flow of history, but she died before I had a chance. It did, however, give me the notion that I should tape the recollections of another member of my family, an aunt named Betty Parsons, who had started an art gallery in New York in the 1940s and pretty much single-handedly—to the horror of her friends and derision of the critics—established Abstract Expressionism as a respected art form.

While researching the New York scene of the 1940s and '50s for an article on my aunt that had grown out of the taping, I interviewed Tatyana Grosman, the owner of Universal Limited Art Editions. Mrs. Grosman's firm was then printing some of the best lithographic work ever produced from original art. Many of the artists she had worked with also happened to be in my aunt's "stable," as she called it, and I wanted to solicit Grosman's view of the Parsons Gallery. Recounting an incident about one of their mutual artists led Grosman to describe how she herself had gone into business in America after escaping with her husband from Nazi Germany. The story fascinated me and, after some additional research, I wrote a second essay, on Grosman. It was at this point that Jeff Weiss, a friend who is second only to da Vinci when it comes to devising projects, suggested that these two essays might form the nucleus of a book about a number of women who had made a lasting contribution to this century.

The notion appealed to me even though it might be considered inappropriate for a man to chronicle and try to understand what enabled certain women to achieve success. However, having been surrounded by successful women all my life—both my mother and my aunt ran galleries, my wife has her own business, and I have worked my entire adult life for a publishing company whose magazines are all edited by women—successful women were the norm to me.

I became interested in what influenced or motivated successful women to enter their chosen professions before there were role models. How did their husbands respond to this show of independence? How did they manage to have a family and a career at the same time? Did their children suffer any ill effects because their mothers were away so much of the time? Was it really worth it for those women when most of their earnings went to child care? Was any one conviction shared by all of them?

Though there were no absolutes, certain patterns did emerge as to what motivated the women to enter their professions. The artists, of which there were four, were driven by a purely spontaneous urge to create. Their families, with one exception, played no positive role. On the other hand, the five doctors interviewed together with two college presidents, were greatly influenced by their parents, were themselves well educated, and steered their children in the same direction. The women in business were much less influenced by their parents and entered their field mainly out of economic necessity. As for law and government, it was their early surroundings that alerted these women to the fact that social and economic equality was not available to everyone, and this awareness drove them to become crusaders. Johnson-Masters and Clarabelle Williams fit no pattern unless one assumes obstacles placed in their path merely strengthened their resolve to succeed.

The results strongly point to the fact that these women's husbands were supportive, and their wives credit a good measure of their success to this. In many cases the husbands were in the same or allied fields. None of the five divorced women became successful until they left the unsupportive mates and struck out on their own or married men of greater understanding.

The great majority chose to have children and a career, and combined the two successfully. Most believe that one should first be established in a career because, if you so choose, you will not only be able to reenter the field after the children are born, but your earning capacity will be sufficient to allow you to employ someone to take care of the children in your absence. This is not to say that all the mothers interviewed went straight from the maternity ward to the office or laboratory; many took years off before they returned. But being established in a profession before having children leaves one's options open. But are those children left in someone else's care harmed? The answer would certainly seem to be no. The President of Barnard and a professor of clinical psychiatry in Harlem both strongly maintain that it is not the amount of time a mother spends with her child, but the quality of the time. Insofar as I have been able to determine, the children of all the women interviewed were successful in their adult lives.

As to the question of whether there was any one shared conviction, there was a clear answer: women should receive commensurate wages with men for comparable work. They were all incensed that women's average pay lagged some 35 percent behind men's.

If my life had been influenced more by women than by men before I began this book, it is doubly true now that I have been exposed to almost 1,600 years of collective wisdom. For each of these women has in her own way taught me something, and collectively they have left an indelible mark upon my conscience. They have taught me that true success is not the companion of ambition, but the child of dedication. That there are no junior partners in successful marriages. That for generations we have been neglecting one-half of the creative potential of humanity by ignoring women's intellect. That women are capable of combining a career and a family and the success of each will therefore be greater. That when the offspring of these women leave home, their careers help fill the void. And that if mankind has become somewhat more humane since the Dark Ages, how much more civilized we might be now if women had been allowed a greater voice in ethical decisions.

WISE
WOMEN

Berenice Abbott

"THE ACT OF CREATING HAS ITS OWN REWARDS AND THEY ARE PRIMARY"

Berenice Abbott has said that because of an unhappy childhood she early on learned self-reliance and became "a very independent kid." This independence never left her, and in fact controlled her destiny. While a childhood that was "totally dead," as she says, tends to build self-reliance, it also tends to make decisions about what to do with one's life more difficult. First she wanted to become a farmer, another time an astronomer, still later a pilot, a journalist, and then a sculptor, before finally settling down to the photography for which she has become famous.

The decision to leave her birthplace, Springfield, Ohio—and as soon as possible—was an easy one, though. At the age of nineteen, with twenty-five cents in her pocket, she left for Columbus to study journalism at Ohio State University. She supported herself as a housekeeper for several semesters until persuaded by friends to continue on to New York to attend Columbia University's School of Journalism. But Columbia was not to her liking and she has referred to it since as "a hell of a sausage factory." Berenice Abbott's speech is not open to misunderstanding, nor

1

are her opinions. Scrappy, fiercely loyal, willing to go to the ramparts in defense of her beliefs, she possesses a public image very close to her private being. Like a good fighter, she is lean, hard, trim, and looks her adversary straight in the eye. In short, she is a woman of spirit. She is also an artist and because of this probably found the life of Greenwich Village more refreshing than the "sausage factory." Here she met Man Ray, Marcel Duchamp, Edna St. Vincent Millay, Eugene O'Neill, and the actors of the Provincetown Playhouse, where O'Neill's plays were then being staged. James Light, who was in charge of the Playhouse, gave Berenice some bit parts until she and the rest of the cast came down with the Spanish influenza, which in 1918 was ravaging the country and Europe. It was upon her recovery that she decided to take up sculpture and leave for Paris to study with Émile-Antoine Bourdelle since she "might as well be poor in France as in New York."

She carried with her a letter of introduction to André Gide, which it was hoped would give her entrée to the artistic and intellectual circles of the Left Bank. In 1921 Paris was the artistic mecca of the world. Pablo Picasso, Henri Matisse, Max Ernst, Marie Laurencin, Marcel Duchamp, Francis Picabia, Jacques Lipchitz, Ossip Zadkine, Naum Gabo, Amédée Ozenfant, Fernand Léger, Robert Delauney, Sonia Delauney, Chaim Soutine, André Derain, Pierre Bonnard, Raoul Dufy, Alexander Rodchenko, Constantin Brancusi, and many others were there. She studied in Paris and Berlin, but then her money ran out and she needed steady employment.

Fortunately her old friend from New York days, Man Ray, needed an assistant, preferably one who knew nothing about taking pictures, and in this Abbott qualified handsomely. She went to work for him in 1923 and immediately fell in love with photography. She never again returned to sculpture. While she claims that her study of sculpture helped in visualizing objects in the third dimension, she nevertheless left it firmly behind her. As the story goes, when she was traveling from Berlin to Paris with a huge block of sculpture, she found herself waiting on the wrong train platform. In her haste she simply abandoned the great stone on the ramp, not once looking back.

She worked in Man Ray's darkroom for three years. "Darkroom work fascinated me [but] I never thought that I would be a photographer. Now that I look back on it, I see how good an assistant I was. I worked hard for him. Man Ray was the first one to say 'Why don't you take some pictures?' and he showed me how to work a camera. Neither of us expected the portraits to be any good and both of us were surprised when they were."

In 1926 she and Man Ray were given a show at the Au Sacre du Printemps gallery for which Jean Cocteau wrote the foreword to the catalog. Her work was praised in the press and Man Ray's was roasted, which was embarrassing to her as she did not want to be thought of as competing with her ex-boss.

There had also been a show at the Salon de l'Escalier in Paris as well as one in Brussels, but for the latter she was never paid. When she met the dealer sometime later and asked for her money he refused, telling her he had kept it because he "did not have the courage to be poor."

It was during these years that she came in contact with another photographer: Jean-Eugène-Auguste Atget. Like Abbott, Atget had pursued a number of careers, including acting, until, at the age of almost forty-two, he took up photography and devoted the remaining twenty-nine years of his life to recording, for the most part, the scenes of Paris. She remembers the first time she saw Atget's work at Man Ray's studio she "sort of exploded. . . . I thought they were great." It was then that she began collecting Atget's work, which would eventually constitute one of our most important photographic collections.

Abbott had been in her own portrait studio at 44 rue de Bac for two years when she asked Atget in 1927 to come and pose for her. Abbott remembers that she wanted to evoke his great weariness and take his picture in the patched clothes he wore while working the streets of Paris, lugging around forty pounds of camera and glass plates. To her surprise he arrived in a handsome overcoat and, to her horror, when she took the portrait to his house a few days later, found that he had died. She once asked Atget why he never took pictures on assignment, to which he responded, "People don't know what to photograph," a statement that would markedly affect the choice of her own direction in years to come. As she has written, "[For Atget] it was the subject that was the important thing," and therefore, in his view it was the artist's responsibility to make the choice.

Upon Atget's death, Abbott moved fast to ensure that his works were preserved, for the concierge of his building was ready to throw them out. The problem was, of course, how to raise the money, and it has been claimed that a young art dealer, Julian Levy, gave her a thousand dollars toward their purchase—a claim that she vehemently denies, saying that Levy never bought an interest in the collection "until a year after I had been there." By that time Abbott was succeeding with her own portrait photography so she no doubt had the earning power to purchase Atget's work. The success of her photographic studio is attested to by the fact that James Joyce, Jean Cocteau, Max Ernst, Marie Laurencin, Marcel Duchamp, Janet Flanner, and André Gide among numerous others came to pose.

In 1928, her work was included in the avant-garde exhibition at the Salon des Indépendants, and by then she was even receiving some attention on this side of the Atlantic through Janet Flanner's articles in *The New Yorker.* She was, in short, becoming famous.

Abbott has written that "portraiture is an exchange between the sitter and the photographer." In the case of James Joyce, who sat for her several times, there was a particularly interesting exchange. She recalls: "Joyce during those years was very poor and had to support his family by teaching Italian to an Englishwoman.

Moreover, he had extremely bad eyesight, having undergone three operations in the preceding few years." So though portraiture demands good light, she had to use natural light because strobes or artificial illumination would have been too strong for him. Joyce even wore his hat to protect his eyes. Whatever she did, it worked because, as the critic Avis Berman has written, "The portrait conveys the elegance and exhaustion of James Joyce's family, including the writer, his wife Nora, and his daughter Lucia, not yet in the sanatorium [with a], power to break one's heart. . . ."

It is something of a wonder that Abbott ever returned to her native land, but she has been quoted as saying, "I'm a real American, born in the Midwest, born in Ohio state, no real links to Europe. My family moved into Ohio about 1812 [where] my grandfather was a schoolteacher; when I was young, I taught, too, and my aunt had a big country store." Abbott believes that one of the most accurate appraisals her work has received was the comparison to the writings of Sherwood Anderson. So Berenice had become "nostaligic . . . a little bit homesick. I came back on a visit in February 1929. I was scared of America, it was so materialistic, but I became terribly excited about New York. . . . It was really an explosion of excitement . . . you can get excited to death here so it just hit me in full force and I thought by God I want to come back here and photograph New York." She returned to Paris, swapped her furniture with Max Ernst for a couple of his paintings, and returned home. Her friends said she was crazy.

In the spring of 1929, she opened a portrait studio at 1 West 67th Street. It was not a great success. As she recalls, "People were at that time going to department stores and getting their portraits for a dollar and they were not used to paying high prices for my kind of work." It did not help her business that six months after her return the stock market crashed. She remembers the date only because she was in the hospital having her appendix taken out. Though she cared little for money, she did have to find a method of supporting herself, if only to go on with her photography. As she says, "I came back not to work here, not even to make a living here, but purely and simply to photograph New York." She was asked by *Fortune* magazine to take a series of portraits of businessmen and by *Life* magazine to document a series of scientific subjects.

In fact, Abbott became a very busy woman. Julian Levy opened a gallery in New York and offered her a show along with Atget and a generally unknown Civil War photographer called Mathew Brady, of whom Abbott had heard in Europe. Levy had become interested in his work, so Abbott, after months of research, found an album of photographs in the War Department in Washington, D.C. Previously Levy had bought some of Atget's photography because he thought the work would win instant recognition but, as Berenice says, "It took fifty years." (In fact, as late as 1966, she made a special trip to Paris to meet André Malraux, then the Minister of Cultural Affairs, in order to convince him that Atget's works were of permanent value. But Malraux wasn't buying and so they had to wait another two years for the Museum of Modern Art to purchase her and Levy's collections for a reported $80,000.)

Other projects came on line, too. The architectural historian Henry-Russell Hitchcock, Jr., commissioned her to travel up and down the East Coast to photograph Civil War buildings for an exhibition entitled "The Urban Vernacular of the Thirties, Forties and Fifties." Thus she gained the necessary experience for the mammoth record she wanted to make of New York City. At about the same time she also made forays into rural America, taking more than two hundred photographs in the South, Ohio, and Pennsylvania.

It is amazing that given the demands of her professional life she had the time and energy to pursue her first ambition of documenting a changing New York: a grail that would cost a considerable amount of money. Abbott had applied for support from the newly founded Museum of the City of New York, as well as from private benefactors, but the Depression was still on and patrons of the arts were as scarce as Republicans who admired Roosevelt. Fortunately, in the fall of 1935 the Federal Arts Project, part of the Works Progress Administration, agreed to sponsor the project, giving her $35 a week, an assistant, and a driver. Abbott confides, "I really think that was one of the happiest moments of my life. Moreover, I had been granted a supervisor's wage because most artists were receiving twenty-three dollars a week. Some of these twenty-three-dollars-a-week artists did amazing things while working for the W.P.A. and it just goes to show the amount of talent we had in America." The Federal Arts Project gave her a completely free hand to photograph what, when, and where she liked. The only time she recalls being restrained was when a supervisor cautioned that nice girls don't go down to the Bowery. She settled this dispute by saying that she wasn't a nice girl, she was a photographer.

For two years Abbott worked on this project and in 1937 the Museum of the City of New York gave her a show called "Changing New York." She was also included in group shows at the Museum of Modern Art as well as in the Brooklyn Museum. New Yorkers were about as interested in her work as the Parisians had been in Atget's. Both were reporting on too familiar a terrain to create much excitement.

The critic Elizabeth McCausland saw what Abbott was about though, and wrote that she had "articulated . . . the dual personality of a great city in which the past lives side by side with the incredible present." Each morning Berenice would take her 8 by 10 camera into the streets and, according to McCausland, "set down in the imperishable fabric of the photographic print the ultimate truth which is the artist's contribution to the history, the artist's perception of the moment translated in terms which definitely capture the spirit of the age. . . ." Sadly, almost half of the places she photographed on this project have since been demolished. One exception is Rockefeller Center, the documentation of which she began as a self-commissioned assignment previous to receiving her grant. But other places live only in the "imperishable fabric of the photographic print," such as Pennsylvania Station, Rhinelander Row, the statuary shop on Water Street, and the beautiful old frame houses of Brooklyn and Astoria.

Abbott has been identified with the "truth-telling" tradition of photography much as are Atget, Matthew Brady, Nadar, and Julia Margaret Cameron. She is fond of quoting Goethe's aphorism, "Few people have the imagination for reality." "It's the realistic image that interests me," she says. In her battle against the painterly photographer, she has written, "Pictorialism means chiefly the making of pleasant, pretty, artificial pictures in the superficial spirit of certain minor painters." Because of this she is no fan of Alfred Stieglitz, although she admits that he has produced over his lifetime five good photographs—hardly a ringing endorsement. "When I returned to New York everything revolved around Stieglitz. I went to his place with open arms and was appalled. I didn't like his work and I didn't like him." But she reserves her real displeasure for another of the canonized—Edward Steichen, who directed the Museum of Modern Art's Department of Photography from 1947 until 1962. She says, 'Steichen is an example of a small person who got in a position of power and used it for his own ends. He ran roughshod over me. He wouldn't give Atget a show at the Modern unless his work was in the museum's collection, so he made me sell him fifty Atget prints for five dollars each. Then he wouldn't show Atget alone, only with Stieglitz, because he said Atget wouldn't hold up."

The government's financial support for her "Changing New York" project was withdrawn in 1939 but by then she had published her book on the subject with a text written by Elizabeth McCausland. The year before she had been awarded a position teaching at the New School of Social Research in New York, but, needing other outlets, she soon struck upon the concept of

8

photographing the laws of science. It had never been attempted before and like most new ideas was met with lukewarm enthusiasm across the land.

She wanted to photograph motion, magnetism, gravity, and similar principals, but the scientists preferred to continue portraying these phenomena with old illustrations. She took courses in chemistry and electricity, all the while trying to convince the scientific community of the educational value of such photographs. The Russians came to her help in 1957 by launching Sputnik, and she was then invited to join the Physical Science Study Committee at the Massachusetts Institute of Technology, a body formed to help create interest in science in high schools. It took eighteen years before her ideas were accepted, but Abbott is nothing if not persistent. Her blue eyes glitter like the iron filings she was later to photograph (demonstrating magnetic pull) when she remembers how coolly she was received. When she wanted to do a book on the forces of electricity, most scientists refused to be associated with her. And when she wanted to demonstrate her work, not even the Bronx High School of Science would hire her. After she finally found a collaborator, his wife stepped in and objected to his working with a woman. But in the end she put it best by saying, "The act of creating has its own rewards and they are primary." She herself has demonstrated this too many times for us to doubt.

In speaking about her years in Paris, Abbott commented to the art critic John Russell, "People were more people . . . there were no rubber stamps among us." What was true of her in 1928 remained true of her in 1968 when at the height of her career she abandoned the overheated art scene of New York for a small cabin by a lake up in Maine. She had visited that state in 1954 while traveling along U.S. Route 1 to document the East Coast.

Documentation has always been center to her work and reflects a belief she described in 1937 in the journal *Art Front.* "Generally," she noted, "the function of photography for communication has not been sufficiently expounded. . . . Its purpose is speaking to the present, but also speaking to the future. . . . Art in the best periods has been documentary as well as aesthetic." Some thirty years later in *A Portrait of Maine* she addresses the question of "speaking to the present, but also speaking to the future," by photographing the Down East life of the lumberjack, the potato farmers, the blueberry pickers, and the fishermen struggling with their lobster traps. To this day she continues to record the reality of Maine with a visual clarity she brings to all her work. She once asked if there was anything more mysterious than reality. Unlike some professionals, artists tend not to retire.

BERENICE ABBOTT

Man Ray, self-portrait, 1922

1898 Born Berenice Abbott, Springfield, Ohio

1917 Attended Ohio State University

1918 Came to New York City

1921 Moved to Paris

1923 Assistant to Man Ray

1925 Established photographic studio at 44 rue de Bac

1926 First photographic exhibit at Au Sacre du Printemps Gallery

1927 Purchased Atget's prints and negatives

1928 Exhibited at the Salon des Indépendants

1929 Returned to New York City and opened portrait studio

1932 Exhibited at Julian Levy Gallery

1934 Began work for architectural historian Henry-Russell Hitchcock

1935 Worked for **Fortune** and **Life** magazines. Received Federal Art Project grant to photograph "Changing New York." Traveled through the South, Ohio, and Pennsylvania taking photographs

1937 Exhibited "Changing New York" at the Museum of the City of New York

1938–1958 Taught at the New School for Social Research, New York City

1944 Published A Guide to Better Photography

1948 Published The View Camera Made Simple

1954 Traveled and photographed the East Coast along U.S. Route 1

1958–1961 Photographed examples of the physical sciences

1968 Left New York to live in Maine. Published A Portrait of Maine

1970–1976 Exhibited at the Museum of Modern Art; Witkin Gallery, New York City; Focus Gallery, San Francisco; Marlborough Gallery, New York City; Lunn Gallery Graphics International, Washington, D.C.

James Joyce by Abbott, 1933

Park Row, New York, by Abbott, 1936

André Kertesz and Abbott, 1981

(Left to right) Rita Hillman, William Lieberman, Abbott, Cornell Capa, 1981

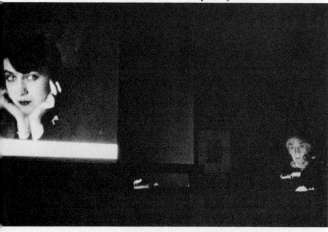

Lecturing at International Center for Photography, November 18, 1981

Anne Belcher

"THE GIFT
OF
COMPASSION"

That crisp fall morning when I first visited Dr. Belcher in her offices on the East Side of Manhattan, the only thing that seemed permanent, within earshot or eye range, was this tiny woman dressed in her starched white doctor's smock, stethoscope dangling from her neck like a piece of pre-Columbian jewelry, examination glasses at parade rest on her forehead, and wearing her gray hair piled high upon her head like a meringue. The structure next door was being demolished by ball and chain, the building across the way was being riveted together, and the street below was being tortured by Consolidated Edison's archeologists in search of ancient cables and worn-out circuit breakers. But Belcher had been in these offices for almost sixty years, ministering to those who suffered hearing problems, and a little commotion outside was not going to change that.

In her hometown of Key Port, New Jersey (population 1,100), where she, the oldest of six children, was born in 1895, construction or demolition was pretty much done by hand, which, if not as efficient, was at least easier on the nerves—and the ears. Our love affair with efficiency helps explain why at last count there were some 16 million Americans with impaired hearing and about 500,000 profoundly deaf. The Greeks not only had a word for it, they had a solution. In the town of Sybaris, some 2,500 years ago, they banned metalworking within the city limits to avoid noise clutter.

Dr. Belcher did not have this in mind when she entered her profession, nor did she consider the fact that the clutter was about to place our eardrums and nervous systems on the line each day. She entered it because two of her aunts were doctors. On a visit from their native Germany, they impressed the five-year-old Anne Seligman as being glamorous. The profession itself took on a fascination that has never faded. Those two sisters, along with Molly Crawford, who was the head physician of the medical department of the Federal Reserve Bank and the first woman to ride shotgun, so to speak, on an ambulance and have her picture in all the New York papers, were all the motivation that this determined girl needed to hie herself over to Cornell at the age of eighteen and never look back. Though the motivation was there, the money wasn't, so according to her daughter Kate, "Mom earned this by picking strawberries."

"One thing any person who enters medicine has to be clear about is that social life, and even child-rearing, must be subordinated to the practice. There will be very little time for parties and the like," Belcher volunteered. She might just as well have added that anyone who takes up medicine gives up, for at least a number of years, what most of us consider the bare essentials of a social life—at least a social life as it exists outside of the classroom, laboratory, and hospital. It is tantamount to entering a monastery, a monastery that can flunk you out. But in some respects, she was luckier than other women who enter medicine, for there were twelve or thirteen other girls in pre-med when she entered in 1913, which she believes to be the high watermark in female enrollment in Cornell Medical School. For even though it is written into their charter that they must accept women, she said, "They can limit it to ten percent, which is what they do now, practically."

Seligman had one other piece of good fortune. While sharing a cadaver with another young intern, he was concerned enough to ask, "Do you think you are going to be able to get through this dissection?" His name was Harold Belcher, and they were married in 1922, right after she finished her internship. She received $25 a month during her residency in Newark City Hospital and Belcher presumably received the same amount for serving his internship at New York Hospital on the other side of the Hudson River. A total of fifty dollars a month, even in 1922, was not going to go far, so they resided in their respective hospitals to save money and simply met on the weekends for the next few years. They were in fact conducting an extended marriage before the term was known. Even now Belcher is not one to be free with her money, for though she has one of the most successful practices in New York, she can still be seen riding the bus to and from work.

During the last six months of her two-and-one-half-year internship at Newark City Hospital, Belcher's compulsory was head and neck surgery, and it was at this time that she became interested in specializing in ear, eye, nose, and throat ailments (known in the profession as otolaryngology). Dr. Wells P. Eagleton, her teacher and the head of the department, had himself, at the age of fifty, just gotten married for the first time, having made the discovery that "women were all right." So apart from their mutual interest in nasal passages, inner ears, and the like, they also had the common bond of being newlyweds. Dr. Belcher remembers him as a "marvelous teacher who went out of his way to make the subject interesting." He was not her last teacher, for medicine is one of the professions that demands regular updating. Ten years after studying with Dr. Eagleton, she went to Vienna for courses on ear pathology with Professor Noigland, where they had the "most marvelous teaching facilities" and access to "all the latest equipment." Also, "In Vienna, at that time, it was compulsory to perform autopsies" so they had, in her words, "plenty of material to work with." If taking courses was one thing that she enjoyed, instructing young interns at New York Hospital (Cornell Medical College) was even more satisfactory, and she continued to do so on a regular basis for nearly half a century.

Anne Belcher probably would have remained permanently as a physician-in-residence at the New York Infirmary for Women and Children, which she had joined in 1923 after graduating from Cornell, if it had not been for a Dr. Connie M. Guion. Dr. Guion is, for physicians, a legendary person. She was the first woman in the country to have been made professor of clinical medicine, the first woman to become a member of the medical board of the New York Hospital, and the first woman to be appointed an honorary member of that hospital. It was Dr. Guion who convinced young Dr. Belcher in 1924 to take the space that she is still sharing with the sounds of the city.

"It would have been much easier to have remained on a hospital staff, with its regular hours and built-in support systems and services, rather than entering private practice, which is in fact like going into business," Dr. Belcher admits. She might also have added that starting a private practice and having a baby in the same year, which is what she did in 1924, is probably not something she herself would recommend to many of her patients, though she maintains that it was "no big deal because the practice was not so large at the time that I couldn't afford to take the time off." Mother, child, and practice all survived. Two years later a second daughter was born and at last count, Dr. Belcher has six grandchildren and one great-grandchild. "Practicing medicine and being a mother never really presented me with any particular problem other than that I could not spend as much time with the girls as I would have liked."

Belcher soon faced the problem that more and more professional women are coming up against today—how to steal time away from a busy career to spend it with the children. If one speculates as to whether the closeness of the family is affected by a mother who is out all day working, the answer in this case would have to be a resounding "No." By every measure this is a close-knit family, for though the two daughters now live on the West Coast, they both hop back and forth across the continent as if they were going to the corner store.

Though Belcher is reticent about discussing why she has become one of the most sought-after doctors in New York City, her patients have no such reservations. Miki Denhof, for many years the Art Director of *House & Garden,* says that she dreads the thought of Dr. Belcher retiring, for "while there are undoubtedly other otolaryngologists to whom I could go, it would be difficult to find any doctor that I would feel more comfortable with." Another of her patients commented, "Anne treats the whole person and not just the sickness." Her daughter Kate put it best when she said, "Mom has the gift of compassion." While all this may be true, the first impression that Belcher makes with her steely blue-gray eyes, angular Gothic American features and wiry build is one of being stern and rather aloof, so to this visitor, at least, it would appear that she has some way to go in engendering a feeling of ease in her patients. "Not so," insists Denhof, "this impression quickly vanishes for she is never in a hurry . . . gives you her full attention and when you are being treated by her you know that at that moment you are the most important thing to her."

What does not appear to be the most important thing to Dr. Belcher is the manner in which she has arranged her waiting room, or to be more accurate, the way she *hasn't* bothered to arrange it. But here again, first impressions are misleading, for it presents an interesting contrast to the chrome, glass, and recessed lighting of many an office. Its plainness creates the impression that you are dealing with someone who is more interested in results than presentation. There could be no other reason for the homeliness of all those assorted straight-back chairs lined up with Grant Wood solemnity against a wallpaper as forgettable as Rosencrantz and Guildenstern. There could be no other reason for the austerity of the square table in the center of the room with those well-fingered magazines (*National Geographic* as opposed to *Geo*) that compete for space with a small lined pad upon which each new arrival must enter his or her name. The order of examination is determined by the sequence on the pad and no one but no one breaks queue or pulls rank in Belcher's office.

The old-fashioned, no-nonsense appearance of her office is an extension of attitudes and opinions formed over the years. A conservative by nature, she is not impressed by the Equal Rights movement, but does firmly believe in women receiving equal pay for equal work. She worries about the younger generation with their "trial marriages and use of drugs," and wonders if the fact that more women are studying to become psychiatrists than pediatricians may not be connected with the "disturbed state of some of our youth." Because she has always imposed discipline upon herself, she finds it difficult to understand the younger generation with its "liberal" attitude toward drugs and sex. She firmly believes that "control of one's physical life is the key to successful relationships and not trial marriages." At eighty-seven she still disciplines herself by conducting her practice from eight in the morning to two in the afternoon. Her waiting room is still filled with patients who have jotted their names down on the lined pad. The only concession that she made to age was to give up surgery at the age of eighty-one.

"You know one of the nicest things that ever happened to me," her daughter Kate confided, "was when a woman came up to me and said, 'You are Anne Belcher's daughter, aren't you? Well, you know, your mother saved my life.' "

ANNE
BELCHER

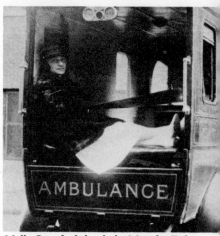

Molly Crawford, head physician for Federal Reserve Bank, riding the ambulance

1895   Born Anne Seligman, Keyport, New Jersey
1913   Pre-med, Cornell College
1920   M.D., Cornell Medical School
1920–1922   Intern, Newark City Hospital
1922   Married Harold Belcher
1923   Consultant in otolaryngology, New York Infirmary for Women and Children
1924–Present   Opened private practice in Manhattan. Continues to practice. Assistant surgeon, Manhattan Ear, Eye and Throat Hospital
Daughter Kate born
Surgery, otolaryngology, New York Hospital
1926   Daughter Suzanne born
1932   Instructor, otolaryngology, Cornell Medical School
1976   Gave up surgery

Belcher with (left to right) granddaughter Kelly Scribner, great-granddaughter Sarah Scribner, and daughter Kate Webster

Belcher's waiting room

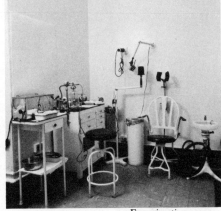

Examination room

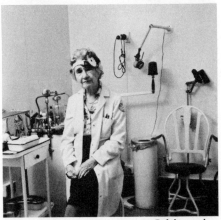

Belcher today

Sula Benet

"IN AMERICA THE INDIVIDUAL IS NOT HELD BACK BY TRADITION"

"Don't you want a drink? Well, at least some coffee or tea and perhaps just a small slice of cake, and be sure and try some of that honey on the pita bread and the gooseberry jam on the cracked rye. The chocolate is delicious, and I insist that you at least try one of the lace cookies."

Dr. Sula Benet sparkles with enthusiasm, and the first thing that becomes clear is that you are in the presence of a giver. Her laugh is like that of a child's. There is no millisecond of hesitation in the voice between the offering and the parting with that proffered. Her gestures are big and generous as though hugging the topic to her bosom. But most of all, her eyes are those of a giver, for they gleam, almost naughtily, in their love affair with life.

The love affair seems to have started early, and to have been approved of by her parents, particularly her father. When she told him that she wanted to attend the university in Warsaw to combine her interest in folklore with that of ethnography, even though she realized that making a living from this discipline was unlikely, her father responded, "You should study what you want

25

for you never know what is going to happen in the future, and how your life will go."

As a silk merchant who traveled widely in the East, her father was obviously able to give his daughter a wider perspective than was available to most of the Jewish community living in Warsaw in the 1930s. It was that same perspective that caused his concern about the future. But Sula grew up in comfortable upper-middle-class surroundings with servants, nannies, tree-lined streets, and parks with Punch and Judy shows. She recalls that many summers her parents would travel to the Caucasus, her father on business, her mother going along to take the waters. "They would return with colorful stories of the wonderful people they met in that land of towering mountains, plunging ravines, and remote villages. They promised to take me there someday and I yearned to go, but it was not to be then." Yet later her most important work would take place in that land of towering mountains.

From earliest childhood Sula Epstein had been fascinated with folk literature, and while attending the Russian School in Warsaw, and later at Warsaw University, she systematically read everything she could find on the subject. "I loved folk literature and wanted to understand why, for example, there are five hundred different versions of the 'Cinderella' story in Europe alone. And how it is that the American Indians have a different version because in their culture there is no emphasis on the stepmother."

The tales themselves raised more questions than they answered. She was intrigued by stories that came from totally unrelated cultures yet bore such marked similarities, and how they were influenced by the civilization from which they sprang. Her graduate work at Warsaw University was performed under Professor Stanislav Poniatowski, and her thesis was on the origin of hashish, as it related to folk customs and beliefs.

She traced the use of cannabis back to the Old Testament by using the original Hebrew text, and found it to be "an integral part of religious celebrations as well as an intoxicant . . . because

26

the aroma was pleasing to the gods." In her paper, "Cannabis and Culture," she wrote that in Exodus 30:23 "God directed Moses to make a holy oil composed of 'myrrh, sweet cinnamon, kaneh bosm [aromatic cannabis] and kassia.' " She traced it back a thousand years before its first mention by Herodotus in the fifth century B.C., back to the Scythians or, as the Semites called them, Ashkenazis, whose progenitor was the great-great-grandson of Noah. From the cannabis seed, hemp was grown, and what was left over, after turning on the Ashkenazis, was made into rope and sold to King Solomon, who ordered "hemp cords among other materials for building his temples."

While still a student at the university, she met Samuel Benet, who was practicing law. Almost half a century later her voice still falters and trails off when she recalls this period of her life. "We were married in 1934 but lived together for less than two years when Samuel suffered a ruptured appendix and died. I was twenty-nine at the time and a research assistant at the Polish Academy of Sciences." A few months later her old Professor Poniatowski suggested that she leave Poland, travel to New York, and take her Ph.D. with the famous Dr. Frank Boas, a pioneer in American anthropology. For Benet, who wanted to investigate the American Indian, the suggestion was fortunate. It was fortunate for her in more ways than she could have imagined, for her mother, her younger sister Ruth, and Ruth's husband, who remained in Poland, were all executed by the Nazis.

Boas had been for the previous thirty-seven years a professor of anthropology at Columbia University, where he inspired generations of students, including Ruth Benedict. When Benet arrived at Columbia, Boas had just retired so she studied with Dr. Benedict. "Benedict was a tremendous influence in my life," Benet says. "In fact, she completely changed my thinking. Up to that time I had been brought up in the historical school of anthropology and couldn't comprehend the evolution of things without relating them to the past. So it was a revelation for me to listen to Benedict and to recognize that culturally conditioned responses make up the greater part of human behavior. Just think how the American personality has been influenced by American culture. There is always the possibility in this country of the push forward; the important thing is that in America the individual is not held back by tradition. Otherwise you couldn't have made the achievements you have."

When Sir Walter Scott met John James Audubon he wrote afterward how the personality of the great painter had been altered by living in the American wilderness. "Audubon," he said, "is an American by naturalization; a Frenchman by birth but less a Frenchman than I have ever seen—no dash, no glimmer or shine about him but great simplicity of manner and behavior . . . simplicity is the prominent characteristic!"

Though she came to this country to study the customs and habits of the American Indian, because of the war and other events, Dr. Benet did not get around to meeting her first Indian for twenty-five years, and by that time she was a leading authority on the culture of Eastern Europe. Because she is fluent in Polish, German, Russian, and several Ukrainian dialects, it is not surprising that her speciality became Eastern Europe instead of the American Indians. It was Dr. Benedict's theory on the manner in which differing cultures arose that had such a lasting influence on Benet. If history was of secondary importance in forming a culture, genes were of even less use, according to Benedict. She theorized that cultural heritage is, "for better or for worse, not transmitted biologically . . . as it is in the social insects . . . which represent nature when she was taking no chances. . . . The queen ant removed to a solitary nest will reproduce each trait of sex behavior . . . and . . . each detail of the nest. The pattern of the entire social structure is committed to the ant's instinctive behavior." For man, she argues, the opposite is true, as "no one item of his tribal social organization, of his language, or of his local religion is carried in his germ cell." In short, cultural patterns are transmitted intellectually and not biologically and a culture is in itself "a personality writ large."

In 1948, Sula Benet and Dr. Benedict traveled to Eastern Europe, where they researched what sort of "personality writ large" the culture of Poland had produced. "[Ruth] remained only three weeks. Because she could not speak the language, I acted as her translator and what amazed me was that though she didn't know a word of Polish, she could guess the answers informants gave before I had a chance to repeat them in English. We shared a large room and in the evening Ruth would write poetry which we would sometimes read in the morning. Much of it was of a religious nature for she was very much taken by the image of Mary. . . . My trip to Poland gave me so much . . . she was such a great influence on me."

Benet also worked with Margaret Mead. "Margaret Mead was a marvelous field worker—perceptive, thorough, and practical. Benedict was a great theoretician. I admired and loved them both, and learned from each one. A great personal friendship developed from working with them." At first she had a hard time studying with Benedict, for the doctor had difficulty with her hearing and had to read Sula's lips which were not, she admits, forming the king's English with Churchillian clarity. She mimics the way she thinks she once spoke. "Ve had our difficulties with Benedict at the beginning because she rad lipz and I did not put my lipz the proper vay, so she really had difficulties to understand me. Then we became great frenz and first I became her azistant and then I vas vorking vith her." Benedict had written that the number of sounds that can be produced by our vocal cords and our oral and nasal cavities is virtually unlimited . . . and a great deal of our misunderstanding of languages unrelated to our own has arisen from our attempts to refer phonetic systems back to ours as a point of reference. They overcame this difficulty, for soon, Dr. Benet says, "I was working with her."

One morning in 1970, as Dr. Benet was conducting her an-

thropology class at Hunter College in New York, a telegram
arrived from the Soviet Academy of Sciences inviting her to come
to Abkhasia in the Caucasus to conduct a study of the collectivization of the farms in the area. Previously she had translated into
English a book on an ethnographic study she had made of a small
Russian village, which was published in New York. The original
book had been written in Russian and published by the Institute
of the Academy of Sciences in Moscow. As Sula explains the
invitation, "The Institute was pleased with my work because I had
not dealt with any of the political aspects of collectivization but
simply wrote a straightforward report on the village itself. When
they asked me to come to Abkhasia I wasn't even sure where that
was, but wired them right back 'thank you coming' and then went
home and looked it up in the atlas." It was not far from the place
where her mother once took the waters and wrote to her about
"the towering mountains, plunging ravines, and remote villages."

"I was invited there," Sula says, "to make a study of the collectivization of villages in the Caucasus, which didn't interest me
much, but what did I care? I wanted to go and remember so well
how it turned my life's work around. I was told to ask questions
of some of the older people about what were the problems
created early on by the collectives. 'You must talk to old so-and-
so,' someone would tell me; 'he's a hundred and four and will tell
you all about what happened.'

" 'One hundred and four? He's senile, there would be no use
to talk to him.'

" 'No, no, he has a marvelous memory and will be very helpful.'

"And so he was. Two weeks later I telephoned the academy
and said 'I don't want to do collectivization, I want to do longevity.'" That was the beginning of Dr. Benet's most important work.
There is much to be said for serendipity.

One of the people she was told she must visit was Khfaf

Lazuria, "a delightful old woman" of 139 years, who sipped vodka and smoked a cigarette while talking to Sula. She was incredulous when Sula declined a drink. But Mrs. Lazuria had earned her midday libation, and as for the ill effects of smoking, she was not overly concerned; she had not taken up the habit until she was a hundred, the same year she had to give up horseback riding because the increasing traffic on the road frightened the horses. In her younger days she had been a midwife and delivered a hundred children. She had been married four times, first at the age of forty (that husband died), then at fifty, this time becoming a Christian (she was born a Moslem), and again when she was 108.

"I remember," Benet said, "that, as we were talking, her grandnephew, Mushni Teavich, an eminent Abkhasian poet, announced that they were expecting another guest, 'the girl my great-aunt married off,' as he put it. To my great surprise, I discovered that the 'girl' had been married off some eighty-three years before, at the age of seventeen. She was now one hundred.

"The three of us had 'girl talk,'" said Dr. Benet, "for I was wearing a number of rings at the time and they both wanted to try them on. They also admired my necklace, and when they spotted my petticoat they asked me to raise my skirt so they could see if it was handmade or done by machine. Those two had the eyes of a shoplifter. When I told Khfaf that I heard she could thread a needle without glasses, she laughed. 'I never wear glasses,' she said. 'What would they do for me?' Oh, yes, she would be glad to thread a needle for me. But we are sitting in the shade so it must be white thread. Her great-granddaughter went into the house and brought out a needle and thread. Khfaf's agile fingers threaded the needle in just a few seconds. She held it up with a flourish. I'd prepared my camera to photograph the actual threading, but she was so quick that I only captured her triumphant look as she pulled the thread through."

The question that resurfaces is, how do we know that these

31

people are really as old as they say? After all, birth certificates were not very common in the Caucasus a hundred or more years ago. According to Dr. Benet, the most reliable method of establishing their age is still intensive cross-examination of the old people themselves and the preparation of genealogical tables. She has prepared charts on long rolls of vellum, like Japanese scrolls, very beautiful to look at, tracing the Abkhasian families back generation by generation. She establishes dates by asking such questions as "How old are you? How old is your son? How old were you when he was born? How old were you during the Revolution? . . . During the cholera epidemic or 1892? . . . At the abolition of serfdom in 1869? . . . At the mass resettlement of the Moslems in Turkey in 1864?" and so on. The answers could be cross-checked in many cases by visiting the archives where baptismal and marriage certificates are kept.

For Sula Benet the most interesting question is not how long these people have managed to live, but how they have maintained a vitality well after most of us, with all the benefits of the twentieth century at our disposal, have long since cashed in. There is, of course, no one answer, but Benet believes that "aside from such gifts of nature as an agreeable climate and genetic good fortune, Caucasians live as long as they do because of the cultural environment which structures their existence." Genetics and diet play a part, but an equally important factor is how these people deal with stress. "They are no more immune to the anxieties of human existence than we are," Benet contends, "but they live in a stable culture that buffers them from the worst effects of these tensions. Every aspect of their lives follows a set pattern from birth to death; there's a place, time, and a stage of life for everything . . . and this helps protect them from the pyschological and organic stresses that are triggered by sudden change. The Caucasian, unlike the American, almost always pursues the same career, whether it is farming or sheep-herding, throughout his life."

Another Abkhasian tradition that may also help to explain why there has never been a case of heart disease or cancer reported among them has to do with their eating habits. According to Dr. Benet, they eat their meals on a schedule that never changes: breakfast at 7 A.M., lunch at noon, dinner at 6 P.M.—and they never eat greasy foods. "You can't find a bowl of soup in the whole territory. They boil a chicken and then throw out the water because any fat is repulsive to them. An analysis of the diet of seventy-eight men and forty-five women, each of whom was a hundred years old or more, showed that 74 percent of their intake was milk and vegetables and that all their lives they had eaten meat and other proteins in moderation."

All this abstinence does not mean that their social life is barren. Far from it. In the summer they set up long tables under the great shade trees in their courtyards and give dinners that last four or five hours, while everybody drinks wine with an alcoholic content of 6 or 7 percent. They put great emphasis on the family as well as the satisfaction of being able to please their guests. They can spend hours toasting one another and are filled with praise for the object of the toast.

"I wish to toast young Michail Bekauri on this his ninetieth birthday. Such a man is a great source of pride to our village, a comfort to his wife, an inspiration to his children, a hero to his friends, a counselor to his brethren, and at his still young age, has already attained a wisdom that one might expect in a much more mature person. . . ."

Hearing this, Dr. Benet asked the toastmaster if he believed everything he was saying about young Michail. The answer was "No, we don't, but if we praise him, he is going to try harder." "You know," she told me, "human understanding is their great achievement."

The Abkhasians have an almost Anglo-Saxon aversion to outward signs of emotion or public displays of physical affection. This modesty extends to their sex life where any such exhibition destroys its special quality—like stripping a flower of its petals

33

and leaving it naked, as one of Benet's friends expressed it. This delicacy extends to married life and into labor and childbirth. "In Abkhasia," according to Benet, "a husband will take his wife to the hospital if she breaks her arm, but never to give birth—that delicate mission is performed by a relative or friend." At the onset of labor the husband leaves the house and does not return until she is completely recovered—the folk expression for it is that he "gets shy."

But there are very strict standards governing the conduct of the younger people and rigid rules in regard to courtship. For example, a "man promises to wait months or longer after the wedding before exercising his sexual rights, in order to demonstrate his strength of character and self-control." In much of the Caucasus, intercourse is often determined by the woman, and it would be considered indelicate for a husband to make sexual advances without receiving some signal or invitation. In some ways this custom can be seen as a demonstration of the laws of compensation, for whereas virginity for a woman before marriage is an absolute necessity, intercourse after marriage is regulated by her wish.

I asked Dr. Benet how she managed to research the sex life of these reticent people who, even among themselves, would not discuss this aspect of their lives. "Well," she said, her eyes beginning to laugh, "that was the hardest thing for me to do . . . men and women do not gossip casually about their sexual relations. . . . I had an assistant . . . a young Abkahasian of about thirty-four, married, with three children and a wife who was a teacher. I wanted a family man so that I could ask all kinds of questions. Anyway, he had a friend in a nearby village, and one day I said, 'Look, let's all take a drive, I have some questions to ask.' So we got in the car . . . they were in the front seat, and I was alone in the back so they could not see my face. I began by saying to them, 'Look, you have been telling me for years now that it is a good thing to get married late. What do you do in a society where women are strictly secluded and where it is difficult to come close to a woman sexually or even socially? You're human, what do you do? What about homosexuality?' They both denied that there was any. 'What about bestiality? What do you do with sheep?' And they laughed and laughed. 'Okay, I said, I have my answer.' "

When Dr. Benet is not riding in the back seat of a sedan asking indiscreet questions of Abkhasians, she is compiling her findings as a senior research associate at the Research Institute for the Study of Man on the Upper East Side of Manhattan. R.I.S.M.'s purpose is the dissemination of knowledge in the behavioral sciences and it conducts investigations into everything from longevity and chronic smoking of cannabis in Jamaica, to the value of children in Thailand. As an institution dedicated to helping humans better understand themselves, it is just the right place for Sula Benet.

SULA
BENET

1906 *Born Sula Epstein in Warsaw, Poland*
19? *Attended Russian School*
1934 *Married Samuel Benet*
1935 *Graduated from the University of Warsaw with a diploma in anthropology*
1936 *Research assistant at Polish Academy of Sciences*
Published **Hashish in Folk Customs and Beliefs**
Samuel Benet died
Emigrated to United States
1938 *Became a U.S. citizen*
1942–1944 *Studied with Ernest Hooten and Alfred Tozzer at the Peabody Museum at Harvard*
1944 *Ph.D., Columbia University*
1944–1946 *Taught courses in cultures of Eastern Europe at Columbia. Worked with Ruth Benedict and Margaret Mead*
1946–1956 *Instructor at Hunter College of the City University of New York*
1947–1949 *Research assistant at Columbia University*
1948 *Visited Poland with Ruth Benedict*
1950–1951 *Teaching instructor at Columbia University*
1951–1956 Published **Songs, Dance and Customs of Peasant Poland** *(1951);* **Patterns of Thought and Behavior in the Culture of Poland** *(1952);* **American Riddle**

Benet as a young woman

Book, *in collaboration with Carl Winters (1954);* **Riddles of Many Lands,** *in collaboration with Carl Winters (1956)*
1956–1974 *Associate Professor at Hunter College of the City University of New York*
1970 Published **The Village of Viriatino, Past and Present** *and* **Festival Menus Around the World**
First trip to Abkhasia
1971–1973 *Full Professor at Hunter College*
1972–Present *Senior Fellow of the Research Institute for the Study of Man. Continues to make trips to Abkhasia*
1974–1976 Published **Abkhasian, the Long-Living People of the Caucasus** *and* **How to Live to be 100—The Lifestyle of the People of the Caucasus**
1982 *Died, November 12*

Benet in Caucasus

Respect for age is an Abkasian hallmark

Shepherding, Dagostan

Abkasian man at 106

Benet in her study

Betsy Blackwell

"THE SYMBOL OF SUCCESS WAS ONCE A LADDER — NOW IT'S A JIGSAW PUZZLE"

Some women like to work, some women need the challenge of work, and some women simply must work to keep body and soul together. For Betsy Talbot Blackwell none of these motivations were present when she asked Dorothy Shaver—the legendary driving force behind Lord & Taylor—for a job as a comparison shopper during her spring vacation back in the 1920s. What did motivate this fifteen-year-old child over from St. Elizabeth's convent in New Jersey for the holidays, was the purchase price of a pair of golden slippers which her working mother couldn't afford to buy.

Today, sixty years later, in her cozy house in Connecticut all encircled by great oak and maple trees, the visitor sits in a living room filled with cabinets crammed with porcelain, glass, silver, silk, and wooden miniatures of shoes and boots that she had collected during her thirty-four-year reign as Editor-in-Chief of *Mademoiselle* magazine. But it was that original pair of golden slippers that primed the pump of her ambition and prodded this 5-foot-2½-inch-packet of energy into action. It has since been said that it was energy combined with iron will that the nuns were first to recognize in this Presbyterian lass who had been sent to them over in Convent Station, New Jersey, that enabled Betsy to recover from scarlet fever. "I remember," she told me, "thinking that if God gives me but one wish it would be good health." Betsy was granted or willed her wish.

When Blackwell's mother, Benedict Bristow Talbot, became a fashion stylist at Lord & Taylor's, it was well before the time women of "gentle birth" had careers, unless forced to do so out of necessity. Mrs. Talbot found herself in just such a position, having recently divorced Hayden Talbot, a writer and dreamer who wandered out of their lives when Betsy was seven years old. Wandered so far that alimony payments almost never caught up, and the child would never see him again. "When my mother divorced my father she wasn't trained for anything . . . had never worked . . . didn't have any experience, but what she did have was a flair for fashion. Most women who could afford it at that time had their clothes made by dressmakers as department stores were only just then beginning to feature fashionable ready-to-wear clothes. Mother knew fashion and she was fortunate enough to be at the right place at the right time." She was also a clothes snob. Blackwell remembers walking along 42nd Street in Manhattan with her mother when she saw a dress hanging in the window of a shabby little shop, and boasted that she could improve on the dress simply by changing the buttons and removing some of the ruffles. Her mother cautioned Betsy not to look at those kinds of clothes as "they will vitiate your taste." Blackwell hastily adds, "It was only afterward that I recognized my mother was saying that I must have a standard." Years later in *Mademoiselle* magazine, she defined good taste as a quality "appropriate to the person, the time, and the place." Blackwell acknowledges that her mother was a "wonderful role model for me." Because Mrs. Talbot was forced to work for a living, to the younger Talbot the idea of going into commerce was completely natural. Unlike many women of her class, it never dawned upon Betsy that a career would not be her destiny and in this respect the relationship with her mother was strikingly like a father-son bond in which the boy is trained to enter the father's business. Years later when she was comfortably married to James Blackwell, she chose work over golfing with the girls, because "one of the most valuable lessons my mother taught me was self-reliance." It must be remembered that this lesson was instilled in an era, to quote *Vanity Fair*, "when fainting was an accomplishment. . . . No girl would have dreamed of a career!" If needed, Blackwell is living proof that once instilled, it is difficult to shake the work ethic.

It was probably this early training that Dorothy Mines, a friend of Mrs. Talbot's, recognized back in 1923 when she offered Betsy a position on a new magazine that Bamberger's, the Newark department store, was starting, to be called *Charm*. The story is that Betsy was on her way to see Edna Woolman Chase, the Editor-in-Chief of *Vogue*, in order to find work on that magazine. She was intercepted in the hallway by Miss Mines, then with the *Vogue Pattern Book*, who swept her into her office and offered a job at the munificent sum of $35 a week, which was just about twice the going rate. Miss Mines had been watching Betsy as she worked for Dorothy Shaver, recognized her worth, liked the cut of her personality, her flair for fashion and, perhaps best of all, her God-given common sense. For this she was willing to back her instinct and pay the premium. Aside from the money, what tempted Betsy was the freedom to help get out a magazine without interference from Bamberger's management, who knew nothing about magazines. They knew what they needed though: a periodical designed to coat the gospel of merchandising with the sugar of good writing and the graceful rendering of drawings, and one that would cater to the public's fascination with the fledgling art of fashion photography. In short, they wanted a magazine with class.

For the next six years—during which Betsy was married, divorced, and remarried—she gave them just such a magazine, and would have gone on doing so if she and her second husband, James Madison Blackwell III, had not produced James Madison Blackwell IV. For the next five years she accepted only special assignments from Tobé, the proprietor of the Tobé Fashion Service—a weekly report on industry trends. Tobé, who was later to co-found the Tobé-Coburn Fashion School, was, along with Betsy's mother, the best-known fashion stylist of the period.

People with an excess of vitality, like B.T.B., as Betsy later became known, need an escape valve or they can sometimes self-destruct. Fortunately for her, another magazine started in 1935, and needed someone to kindle its fire. The first issue of *Mademoiselle* was so bad it was recalled. As Betsy said, "Youth was a five-letter word." Aimed at young women (before youth had any status), it contained fiction and poetry (not a young woman's highest priority), was published by Street & Smith (which up to then had only published pulp like "The Shadow" or "Nick Carter"), and was launched during the height of the Depression. It was also given a name that almost nobody outside of New Orleans could pronounce.

Betsy took one look at it and explained to the businessmen a basic fact of publishing life: almost no one advertises in a magazine devoted exclusively to fiction and poetry. If they hoped to attract advertisers they would simply have to broaden their appeal . . . that is, if they were interested in making money. They were.

So Betsy took over as Fashion Director and Beauty Editor. To give these departments the importance each deserved, the management gave her not only two titles but two names. As the Fashion Director she was listed on the masthead as Betsy Talbot Blackwell, and as Beauty Editor she went under the name of Elizabeth Rich. This simple device served to dress up the masthead by increasing the number of editors listed, and did so at no extra cost—management was already proving its interest in making money. In her first issue of April 1935 she pointed the editorial in the direction of Seventh Avenue and the cosmetics industry, initiating one of the first select-market magazines, and within a few years the red ink turned black. She accomplished this by creating, in her own words, "fashion news that was news and didn't make a dress allowance look silly . . . because a magazine dedicated to youth had a certain responsibility to it."

On the tenth anniversary of her editorship, and six years after she had been named Editor-in-Chief, B.T.B. wrote that *Mademoiselle* had a moral obligation to its readers to make sure that the "whole complicated business of merchandising ran a sane and even course and that the fashions were delivered to the stores in time to be available when the magazine appeared on the newsstand." It was a service magazine, "not a bread-and-butter service magazine, but one with a little wild strawberry jam on it," she said.

Wild strawberry jam needs sugar to bring out the flavor and her sugar was humor. In the very first issue for which she was responsible she set the tone by introducing Helen Hokinson's cartoons as well as humorous pieces on such subjects as "Why a party is a man's worst enemy." She would be the first in this country to publish Saul Steinberg, and a quarter of a century later she turned a whole issue of the magazine over to the editors of the *Harvard Lampoon,* who were not content only to parody its fashion and beauty pages but also had the temerity to burlesque its essays and poetry with such irreverencies as an "Ode to a Tube of Toothpaste (after John Keats)":

> Thou still unopened tube of Kolynos
> Thou cylinder of yet unlathered paste . . .

It must be admitted that the lads down from Cambridge had only the best to burlesque for *Mademoiselle* was so awash in advertising it could afford William Faulkner, Dylan Thomas, Joyce

Carol Oates, and Robert Penn Warren. She could afford to suggest that Truman Capote write about his childhood Christmas experiences in the South, from which idea *A Christmas Memory* sprung, and first appeared in *Mademoiselle,* December 1956. (For the December 1946 issue, Katherine Anne Porter wrote a piece entitled *A Christmas Story,* so it is possible that Capote substituted "memory" for "story.") The editors had Sylvia Plath as a guest editor. The list of authors that B.T.B. published during her reign reveal the great sympathy she felt for the arts along with an understanding and ability to recognize talent. In the 1940s there were Ray Bradbury, Robert Penn Warren, W. H. Auden, and Colette. In the 1950s there were Elizabeth Hardwick, Carson McCullers, Lesley Blanch, Eudora Welty. In the 1960s there were Edward Albee, Gore Vidal, Isaac Bashevis Singer. In the seventies there were Rebecca West, Susan Brownmiller, Hortense Calisher, and Joyce Carol Oates.

Blackwell also brought to the magazine her mother's legacy in that "from the beginning *Mademoiselle,* pronounced Milly, always believed in careers for women." But when it comes to feminist causes she might be considered reactionary. In *Mademoiselle's* fortieth anniversary issue she wrote, "We aren't feminists crusading for women's right to work or battle-axes encouraging competition with our men (the tough-as-tacks career girl is a fast-fading memory, and good riddance). We're realists suggesting how to use your talents and training to meet higher living costs, serve the best interest of your family and community, round out your way of life." In an article in *The New York Times* in 1971 Angela Taylor wrote, "Possibly the only quarrel her staff which, politically, is mainly liberal, has with B.T.B., is her staunch Republicanism. . . . She was founder of a group called Republican Women in Industry . . . has been friends with prominent party members such as the late Governor Thomas E. Dewey with whom she used to play poker and who was her legal adviser."

Always the team player, though she prefers playing captain

(Leo Lerman, a contributing editor to *MLLE,* referred to her as "a benevolent despot in the old-fashioned sense"), B.T.B. is the first to acknowledge that much of the credit for the exceptional talent *Mademoiselle* attracted was in great measure the result of editors like George Davis (who was originally with *Vanity Fair*), Mary Cantwell (later to become a member of the editorial board of *The New York Times*), Cyrilly Abels (Katherine Anne Porter's future literary agent), Marguerita Smith (the sister of Carson McCullers), Leo Lerman, and Edie Raymond Locke, whom she trained as her successor. But for a large proportion of *Mademoiselle*'s readership, it was not so much the short stories as the fashion and beauty pages that attracted their attention. *MLLE* was after all a service magazine, and for these departments Blackwell gathered a remarkable group of young editors. She may have been thinking of how complicated publishing had become when she wrote, "The symbol of success was once a ladder—now it's a jigsaw puzzle."

BETSY
BLACKWELL

Blackwell as a young woman

19–? Born Betsy Talbot, New York City

1921 Comparison shopper for Lord & Taylor

1923 Graduated from Academy of Saint Elizabeth, Convent Station, New Jersey

1923–1930 Assistant Fashion Editor and Beauty Editor of **Charm** magazine

1925 Married Bowden Washington

1929 Divorced Bowden Washington

1930 Married James Madison Blackwell III

1930–1935 Worked for Tobé Fashion Service

1931 Son James Blackwell IV born

1935–1937 Fashion Director, **Mademoiselle**, Street & Smith Publications

1937–1971 Editor-in-Chief, **Mademoiselle**

1959–1961 Member of President's Committee for Employment of the Physically Handicapped

1962 Board member of Street & Smith

February 1966 gate-fold feature showing 25 years of fashion

Blackwell at Mademoiselle

Cover, February 1965

Cover, July 1961

Cover, February 1970

Eleanor Brown

"A CRAZY IDEA"

Interior decorating became a professional trade around the turn of the century—or about ten years after Eleanor Brown was born. The first book on the subject, *The Decoration of Houses*, published in 1897, was written by Edith Wharton and Ogden Codman, and the first true professional in the field was one Elsie de Wolfe, who will also be remembered as the first woman to allow her hair to be dyed blue. This relatively new profession was started by American women and pretty well dominated by them until after the Second World War. It is in fact such a new profession that there are still living members of the guild who were present at its big bang. Elsie de Wolfe, Nancy McClelland, Rose Cumming, Diane Tate, Marian Hall, Margaret Owen, and Eleanor Brown were all in the first wave, and Eleanor Brown is still up front when it comes to making decisions at the decorating firm of McMillen, Inc., which she founded in 1924.

It would be hard to find a woman with a more American background than Mrs. Brown, and her family history tells us something about our own development as a country. Back in

1890, the year she was born in St. Louis, Missouri, her family was manufacturing iron stoves called Magic Chef (still about the best on the market), and antique furniture had the same cachet for the rich as a used car has for us today. Yet sixty years later, she was in charge of seeing that only the best of Italian and French antique furniture was installed in the houses of automobile magnates who had come to realize that a Louis XV *fauteuil*, though used, was not quite the same as a Chevy with 100,000 miles on it.

Eleanor Brown (née Strockstrom) remembers the St. Louis of her childhood, where she would walk to the big private school of Mary Institute in the winter "throwing ice balls at the boys." And she remembers the sweltering summers when the heat was so intense that the British Consulate, operating as the Foreign Office did in India, allowed its civil servants to retreat to the mountains. She and her brother and two sisters either joined their family in Europe or went to their summer place in Minnesota to escape the heat. She remembers the Stanley steamers frightening the horses and the blast of the steam whistle from the side-wheelers as they eased away from the docks to push up the Mississippi to the Missouri and out into a west where twenty-five years earlier Custer had lost his life. She remembers the St. Louis Fair of 1904 ("Take Me to St. Louis, Louis, Take Me to the Fair") where high-button shoes, hoop skirts, and straw bonnets were being escorted by cowboy boots, leather chaps, and ten-gallon hats.

In 1908 she went east to Briarcliff College and met her first husband, Drury McMillen, an engineer with an adventurous turn of mind who swept her down to the forests of Brazil to live amid the "lungs of the planet." Here she got to decorate her first house. It was a grass hut with a hole in the center of the roof which allowed smoke from the open pit fire to escape. There were no Magic Chef stoves for this bride. Drury McMillen had been sent into the interior to construct bridges and roads along with a crew of forty, and Eleanor's task was to cook for them. As her longtime assistant Ethel Smith remarked, "It is difficult to imagine Mrs. Brown riding through the jungles of Brazil on horseback —their only means of transportation—living in a shack and cooking three meals a day for a crew of roughnecks."

After that, life in New York, to which she returned with her son in 1920—Drury remained behind and they divorced in 1923—was understandably boring, but Mrs. McMillen fought boredom not with ladies' luncheons but by taking classes at the Parsons School. She so impressed the head of the school, Frank Alva Parsons, that he suggested she go into business for herself—advice usually not handed out with most sheepskins.

She worked for a year with Elsie Cobb Wilson—another decorating firm—before approaching her father for backing to enter into her own business. He gave her the money on the condition that she would take a bookkeeping course because, he is reported to have said, "If you can't read your own books you can't conduct a business." To this day, according to Irene Booth, a principal in the firm, Mrs. Brown writes all the checks and "dislikes delegating that responsibility even when on vacation. . . . She keeps a tight rein on the business . . . she is very concerned with the figures."

Once McMillen opened in 1924 an intimate collaboration began between it and Parsons, probably the most respected school of its kind. The firm was to transport the school's theories "out there" and into the living spaces of those who could afford the freight and had a taste for formality. What Parsons was preaching Eleanor Brown was practicing. Later she was made a trustee of the Parsons School, which by now was located in both New York and Paris, and together with its president, William Odom, they preached the gospel of the directoire style; she preached it so successfully that the French made her a member of the Legion d'Honneur. As Billy Baldwin, who is certainly among the most creative and articulate interior decorators this country has ever produced, says, "Eleanor should be considered not only an interior decorator but also, and perhaps even more so, an interior architect, for her instinct for interesting use of space is uncanny." He mentions, for example, the dining room she created by turning a humdrum rectangular room into an oval sphere of such perfect scale that it is said not only a Parsons would have approved but so also might a Palladio or a Piranesi.

But, like some plastic surgeons, the work Eleanor Brown is most proud of is not necessarily the facelift, but rather the total restoration of American houses headed toward ruin, such as the Rosedown Plantation in St. Francisville, Louisiana, or Washington Irving's house in Tarrytown, New York. Rosedown was one of those great mansions built near the river before the Civil War which were later to become known as the "Ghosts along the Mississippi." McMillen, Inc., spent six years restoring this house —once they got rid of the snakes and spiders. The research alone took a lot of the time, but what took even more time was the removal, layer by layer, of paint, plaster, and wallpaper until they excavated back to the original Zuber paper that John James Audubon knew when he taught painting to the children of Rosedown one hundred years before. Today Rosedown is rightly a museum.

Given her interest in architecture, it surprised no one when in 1936 she married an architect, Archibald Brown. Among the houses Brown had designed was one for himself on the south shore of Long Island in which they lived for two years until the hurricane of 1938 washed it out to sea. Secretly it is believed that Mrs. Brown was not the least bit unhappy about this act of God as she had discovered a small theater near the village of Southampton that her husband had built some years earlier for a Mr. Ling; she knew just what to do with the property if it ever came up for sale. It did. As Ethel Smith said, "Mrs. Brown had to do a lot of talking to convince her husband that she could turn a theater, complete with a pipe organ, into a workable house." In time she prevailed, sold the pipe organ for almost as much as they paid for the house, and ended up with a place that would be photographed for shelter magazines time and again as an example of originality and charm. The way in which she was able to convert a theater into a house when nobody else could see its potential is the measure of Eleanor's ability to solve decorating problems.

Mrs. Brown has retained the Midwestern characteristic of the laconic understatement. An interview with her is a bit like peeling the paper off the Rosedown walls; information comes off in little pieces. For example, I had been told that somehow Mrs. Brown kept McMillen open with a staff of about ten all during the Depression. I asked how that was possible.

"We built miniature model rooms."

"Why?"

"To give people work."

"How did this come about?"

"Well, Grace Fakes, who taught me at the Parsons School and was now a part of McMillen, brought the idea to me one day, and it seemed better than sitting around twiddling our thumbs."

"How many did you make?"

"Fourteen."

"What size were they?"

"One and a half inches to the foot."

"Who designed them?"

"We did."

"Who built them?"

"We did."

"Who paid to have them built?"

"We did."

"Were they built to be sold?"

"No."

"Tell me about them." And then a big area of paper comes off the wall all in one piece.

53

"Well, after we designed and built them, we had to make the furniture, weave the Aubusson rugs, fashion the crystal chandeliers, hang the curtains, render the miniature pictures, set in the blinds, make lamps and wall brackets, place the bathroom fixtures, arrange the china wherever it was needed and . . . [here she draws a breath] then we sent them around the country with the Junior League on exhibition."

"Are you telling me that you paid a staff of ten all during the Depression just to sit around making dollhouses? Did anyone think that was a crazy idea?"

"They were model rooms, not dollhouses, and it was better than twiddling our thumbs, but maybe it *was* a crazy idea."

"But how did McMillen meet the payroll?"

"We just lost money. Later on though," she adds, "the architectural firm of Delano and Aldrich did take up the idea and made dollhouses which they sold and for which we were commissioned to make the furniture—for these we were paid."

But McMillen also occasionally received some commissions, for they realized that F.F.F. (the trade code name for fine French furniture) was not going to be greatly sought after in F.D.R.'s land of the W.P.A. Drawing on her ingenuity and adjusting to the time, Eleanor Brown helped people decorate inexpensively with fabrics such as Bemis bagging (from which laundry bags are made), mattress ticking, and cotton bunting.

But above all, what probably created the success of her company after the Depression was her integrity. When times got better, and people could consider once more the idea of hiring a decorator to do their houses, they came back asking her and McMillen to help them. Maybe some of those five thousand or so who saw the miniature rooms that she had made to help keep her employees busy had decided that they coveted a lifesized model. Maybe it was not such a crazy idea after all.

ELEANOR BROWN

Brown as a young woman

Eleanor and Archibald Brown

1890 Born Eleanor Strockstrom, St. Louis, Missouri

1908 Graduated from Briarcliff College, New York

1910 Married Drury McMillen

1910–1920 Lived on and off in Brazil

1917 Son Louis born

1920 Returned to New York

1923 Divorced Drury McMillen

1924 Opened McMillen, Inc.

1930 Degree from Parsons School of Design

1936 Married Archibald Manning Brown

1950 Named Chevalier de la Legion d'Honneur

1956 Received medal for distinguished achievement from Parsons School of Design

Southampton theater converted into a house

Living room in Brown's New York apartment

Rosedown after restoration

Brown and Walter Hoving, publication reception for book on McMillen Inc.

Mary Ingraham Bunting

"A SOCIETY GETS THE KIND OF EXCELLENCE IT VALUES"

—John Gardner

Rumor has it that when Mary Ingraham Bunting was being interviewed for the presidency of Radcliffe College she startled the trustees by asking them, if she were chosen, would it be permissible to bring her cow to Cambridge. They might have been even more surprised had they known that this slender woman with cropped gray hair with bangs, hazel eyes (which she insists are mud-colored), a whimsical sense of humor, and an original turn of mind was thinking of accepting the presidency not because she was all that intrigued with the position, but because it afforded her an opportunity to develop some ideas she had formed on the inconsistency of offering women higher education and then depriving them of the opportunity to take advantage of its benefits.

Mary Ingraham was educated as a scientist and therefore taught to ask questions. But the question of what might be done about the problems women face in combining career and family did not arise as a result of her own experiences, because she seems to have led something of a charmed life. Along with two

59

younger brothers and a younger sister, she was born into a well-to-do family that divided its time between Brooklyn in the winter and Northport, Long Island, in the summer. Her father was a lawyer as well as a trustee of Wesleyan and Adelphi College, and her mother was the President of the Brooklyn Y.W.C.A., of the National Board of the Y.M.C.A., a member for thirty years of the New York Board of Higher Education, one of the three founders of the U.S.O., and the first woman to receive the Presidential Medal. When Dr. Bunting studied how genetic and environmental factors affect the growth and behavior of organisms, it might have struck her as fortuitous that both genes and environment had been tailored rather to her advantage. It might have also struck her as an excess of genetic conditioning that all her siblings had, like their father, become lawyers or married them.

In biological terms, she was the family variant who chose a career in science, observing how the appearance and behavior of related organisms grown under the same conditions, but in a culture of slightly different "media," will yield quite different results. In her case, the slightly different "media" would seem to have been brought about by the fact that during her adolescence she suffered from ill health and did not attend school. This early "nontraining" gave her, she believes, the advantage of intellectual independence. "One has an opportunity to discover the satisfactions that come from pursuing one's own interests, and perhaps," she said, "that is why my own early career decisions were guided more by my interest than by any particular ambition." For the rest of her life she would make some key decisions for reasons of intellectual interest and while there was always a rationale behind her choice, it was, as in the case of accepting the presidency of Radcliffe, not always the most obvious reason. For example, after graduating from Vassar in 1931, where she majored in physics, Ingraham went on to the University of Wisconsin for graduate work in agricultural bacteriology and agriculture, not because she was interested in any of the applications of her research but just because of the "intriguing state of ignorance surrounding the subject." How did thousands of different kinds of bacteria cells, which up to that time weren't afforded the dignity of even having nuclei, "manage to reproduce themselves so rapidly and accurately?" Her doctoral thesis was on yellow microbacteria and the pigment carotene—an organic compound that imparts to flowers their red, yellow, and orange colors as well as being a source of vitamin A in carrots and other vegetables. "For me it was a period of discovery," she says, with just a hint of nostalgia. But she also made some discoveries of a more personal nature while at the university, in the form of Henry Bunting, whom she met in his father's pathology class. "Later," she reported, "we skate-sailed on Lake Mendota in the winter, banded birds on the Wisconsin highlands in the spring, and shared Dr. Bunting's pathology course in between." They were married three years later in 1937 after Henry had finished his internship at Johns Hopkins Hospital, and she had earned her Ph.D. in the field of microbiology and taught for a year at Bennington College in Vermont.

Bennington had been established in 1935 as a liberal arts college for dancers, painters, and musicians rather than scientists, and oddly enough it was this that interested Bunting in the job. As she recalls, "Nobody went to Bennington to go into science . . . but I wasn't concerned with developing people into scientists. I was interested, however, in teaching people science as a part of a liberal arts course so as to help them have an appreciation of what the subject was all about. What fascinated me was . . . trying to get people into little research problems which would whet their appetite for the discipline."

Her "little research problems" abandoned the old formulas of having students count the number of stamens in a flower or vertebrae in a cod's backbone, replacing them with experiments more interesting to the undergraduates, such as determining how many left-footed students there were on the campus, or whether spiders could hear. She maintains that "the basic thing is starting people on projects, and genuine projects that would lead to discovering something that nobody else knew." Her methods worked, because a good many students decided to turn to science, a decision usually made at the high school level rather than in college.

It was about this time that she began to investigate a bright red bacterium called *Serratia marcescens* which was capable of producing a variety of pink and white mutants. (During the Middle Ages when such blood-red *Serratia* appeared on communion bread, they acquired religious significance and were known as the Miracle of the Bleeding Host. Today they are called mold.) These scientific experiments as well as her own teaching experience led her to provocative theories concerning the validity of some of the hypotheses upon which our educational system is based. In a lecture she delivered in 1971 before the American Society for Microbiology, she said that she doubted that there was "any discipline that provides a better understanding of the interplay of genetic and environmental factors on growth and behavior than microbiology. In working with microbes one gets intimate feelings for growth curves, population pressures, selectivity, genetic stability, and variation," as well as "a host of other phenomena that cannot help but open one's mind to possibilities in education which one might otherwise fail to consider. Above all, one learns to live with ignorance. If it is so difficult to find out why pigmented variants of *Serratia* survive better than those lacking pigments . . . and if one's best guess proves wrong so often when one *can* test them, one becomes cautious about educational hypotheses which cannot yet be put to the test.

"Take one simple example: To distinguish or compare two related organisms, the microbiologist first cultures them in a series of different media under otherwise identical conditions and observes the appearance and behavior of the resulting populations. This, however, is too often the last thing that the educator is encouraged or permitted to do. Rather, people argue for generations about the relative capability of blacks and whites and boys and girls without ever attempting to grow them under the same conditions. If they really believe that significant differences exist, and it would seem to me surprising if they do not, then why not settle the question . . . and then turn to the more important question which is, 'Given the differences, if any, what if anything should be done for the average woman or for the woman with special talents and interests?' The fact that society has chosen not to offer the same opportunities or to give the encouragement to both sexes (or to members of different races) suggests something far more sinister—a deep fear of the results." Five years later in the *Princeton University Quarterly*, she may have been hinting at the results which these "sinister" motives, "if any," could produce when she wrote: "Contrary to what the founders of this country hoped, education, instead of being an equalizer, *can* keep increasing the gap between the privileged and the underprivileged. If the opportunities do not fit the people's needs, or are not available to them, they fall further and further behind." She is fond of quoting John Gardner's remark, "A society gets the kind of excellence it values." She is also fond of quoting Louis Pasteur's observation that "chance favors the prepared mind."

In 1938, after she and her husband moved to Bethany, outside New Haven, she was almost immediately offered a job at Yale. "When we went up to New Haven, in 1938—if that is the year of the hurricane—" she states with New England crispness, "my husband was associate professor in the Pathology Department at Yale and I wanted to do research." But it was difficult to find a position until Professor Leo Rettger, who was interested in her ideas and in her "prepared mind," gave her a job transferring some acidophilus cultures; her salary was $600 a year but she had free use of the laboratory. He in effect gave Bunting a postgraduate fellowship and permitted her to continue studying color variations in *Serratia*. "I was certainly fortunate for it was not a privilege that many women enjoyed," she stated.

Because, as she says, she wasn't very ambitious, the idea of leaving Professor Rettger's laboratory after two years and retiring to the country for the next six to raise four children, cultivate a large vegetable garden, tend bees, and raise goats and a cow like the one she threatened to bring to Cambridge, probably didn't cause her any anxiety. But serendipity was not going to allow Mrs. Bunting to end her days down on the farm. It offered the unexpected discovery that she liked administrative responsibilities and all their nitty-gritty details, which can be anathema to some intellectuals.

As the story goes, the township of Bethany was considering the possibility of building a regional high school and Mrs. Bunting volunteered to help organize the project. Looking back on those years from the vantage point of her yellow Victorian house in Cambridge enclosed by a picket fence and surrounded by a garden that is laid out in as orderly a fashion as her mind, she speaks of voluteerism as perhaps one of the best ways to acquire skills that might otherwise not be readily available. "As a volunteer I worked very hard in helping develop the school. I had to go through the experience of speaking at town meetings and trying to get the bond issues through and hiring, as part of a small group, the architects and the principal and teachers, and through that I got a lot of administrative experience."

In 1955, a year after her husband's death, she was left to raise three boys and a girl, aged seven to fourteen and this experience became of value. Having remained on the periphery of academic circles during the eighteen years they had lived in Bethany, and continuing to lecture, first at Wellesley and later at Yale, her reentry on a permanent basis to the rarefied atmosphere of academia was not difficult. As luck would have it, Douglass, the women's college of Rutgers, needed a dean, and though it had never occurred to her to apply for the position, it did occur to

Louis Jordan, who had taught at Bennington during her tenure there and had later gone on to be president of Rutgers. "Louis always says that I was his invention as a college administrator," and as things turned out, the invention was successful.

It was during her years as dean of Douglass College that she began to address seriously the question of what could be done to help women who had gone to college, achieved good marks, aimed for honors, but, once having graduated, were rarely able to put to good use the knowledge they had worked so hard to attain. It appeared to her that for many women college was only for college's sake, and while the purist might argue that a good education was a noble end in itself, it was a confusing situation for the women involved and a woeful loss of talent for the nation. The dilemma, she recognized, stemmed from the conflict of how to combine a demanding career with the duties of rearing a family.

"The married women were not the only ones that I cared about, but it seems to me that until you solved this problem for the young married women, the next generation was going to be faced with the same dilemma. I wanted to help people who had ability but were stymied." New ideas, she believed, have a better chance of being accepted in other institutions if they are generated from Radcliffe because of its reputation and the fact that it has a lot of visibility." (She became President of Radcliffe College in 1960.) As she says, "If you were of the conviction that it was essential to change the climate of the country, then the best place to start would be at Radcliffe, where people would probably pay attention. That is to a great extent why I took the job. Our timing was good. In 1960, when we announced the establishment of the institute, the Sunday *New York Times* gave us a front-page story which had tremendous impact. The response from the article was so great that we had to add a special person to answer the telephone and handle the mail.

"The institute's first program for independent studies offered fellowships—their size depending on the need—to women who wished to use their talents in a productive way. The idea was to allow women who were living at home to be able to afford such mundane services as baby-sitters or part-time help so they could continue to work on the subjects in which they were interested. We supplied each of them with a studio or appropriate place to study without interruption, and access to the Harvard libraries and to any courses that they chose to audit. The exciting thing was that these women who had been stuck at home, and not recognized by society as having important contributions to make outside the home, now had a chance. For example, there was a lawyer who had been home with her children and during the time had been developing a knowledge of South American law about which she wished to write a book. By the time she was finished, a number of prestigious law firms competed for her services. But all the candidates were not limited to women with doctorates. Anne Sexton, who was later to win the Pulitzer Prize for Poetry and had never gone to college, was given a grant the first year by the institute. We had artists, writers, historians, political scientists, musicians, a child psychiatrist, and even a pediatrician."

Perhaps only a person who makes the statement "I don't think I was ever very interested in my career" can be selfless enough to set about "changing the climate of the country." For the ambitious, failure can be a terminal disease, and while it may be no fun to the idealist, it is at least usually not fatal. If the 1960s were given to questioning some of our most cherished beliefs and perceptions, then the questions that Dr. Bunting raised about women's continuing education and its effect on our society must be viewed as among the most far-reaching though perhaps the least-heralded accomplishments of that decade.

MARY
INGRAHAM BUNTING

Walking in Wisconsin, 1934

1910	Born Mary Shotwell Ingraham, Brooklyn, New York
1931	A.B., Vassar College, physics major
1932	M.A., University of Wisconsin (agricultural bacteriology)
1934	Ph.D., University of Wisconsin
1936–1937	Instructor, Bennington College
1937	Married Henry Bunting, M.D.
1937–1938	Biology Instructor, Goucher College
1938–1940	Botany Lecturer, Wellesley College
1941–1948	Daughter Mary born, and sons Charles (1943), William (1945), and John born (1948)
1946–1947	Botany Lecturer, Wellesley College
1948–1955	Bacteriology Lecturer, Yale University
1954	Dr. Henry Bunting died
1955–1959	Dean of Douglass College
1960–1972	President of Radcliffe College (1964–1965 on leave to Atomic Energy Commission) Biology Lecturer, Harvard College
1972–1975	Assistant to President of Princeton University for Special Projects
1979	Married Clement A. Smith, M.D.

Bunting and baby

Radcliffe pamphlets

Bunting with her children

Bunting's Harvard freshman seminar in biology, November 1960

h daughter Mary, Inauguration Day, Rad- e, 1960

Radcliffe

Radcliffe demonstration in the 1960s

Bunting, Radcliffe, 1972

Toni Frissell

"TO CATCH EMOTIONS AND FREEZE THEM FOR ALL TIME LIKE A ROSE IN A CAKE OF ICE"

The need for adventure is not a male prerogative. Isabel Burton loved it, Amelia Earhart lived it, Isabelle Eberhardt was destroyed by it, Freya Stark made a profession of it, and Toni Frissell has spent a lifetime tracking adventure with her camera. Antoinette Montgomery Frissell was quite incapable of accepting the quiet, comfortable, upper-class existence that she could easily have enjoyed all her life. She could have watered at Newport each summer, sunned in Palm Beach each winter, tended her rose garden by the 1690 house she shares with her husband on Long Island and in between times taken those same trips to the Ritz in Paris or Claridge's in London that were so dear to the hearts of her contemporaries.

She started life at 113 East 56th Street in New York City, sharing a silver spoon with Nelson Rockefeller in kindergarten, and went on to Chapin, the Lincoln School, and Miss Porter's School in Farmington, Connecticut. But the sheltered Victorian childhood of high-button shoes, white pinafores, and a bonnet trimmed in pink bows that prevailed in Newport before the First

71

World War bears no relation to the Air Force boots, fatigues, and goggled helmet she would don thirty-odd years later during the Second World War.

There is a sneaking suspicion among men that any woman who chooses a life of adventure really would prefer to be a man, but if this is ever true it is certainly not the case with Frissell. She simply wanted the freedom that men enjoyed by going off on "risk-taking trips." The greatest influence in her life and the person who introduced her to these trips was her giant older brother, Varick (Toni is exceptionally tall herself), who took her down to Mexico in 1928 where he was filming the Mexican Revolution for *Pathé News*. Nothing much happened, but just the excitement of hiding in a boxcar near the front lines and waiting for the revolutionaries to make their move was a lot more diverting than sitting around Bailey's Beach Club in Newport. She had a second brother, Monty, who was killed mountain climbing at Chamonix, France, but it was Varick who was and has always remained her idol. She remembers as a child in Newport sitting at sundown on the rocks overlooking the Atlantic and listening to Varick sing in his rich baritone voice—"a voice that was the stuff of operas." She remembers envying him the trips he took to photograph seals off Newfoundland, she remembers imitating his style of photographing with natural light, and she remembers almost dying when he was lost at sea. He had gone back to Newfoundland to document the icebergs, and in order to obtain some dramatic footage had placed kegs of gunpowder on board to blow up the great ice masses and photograph them as they plunged into the North Atlantic. But it was the ship, the *Viking*, instead of the icebergs, that blew up. This happened only two years after Monty was killed and scarcely a year after her mother had died of leukemia.

To save her sanity, Frissell began to take up photography in a serious way. She started at *Vogue*, first writing captions and then in the art department choosing pictures and taking some of her own on the side. It was the ones she took on the side that turned her life around when Condé Nast, *Vogue*'s publisher, came across them. He handed her a Rolleiflex and sent her off to photograph her peers in Newport. Though Nast liked her work, it was really Dr. Agha (the Art Director of *Vogue*) and Frank Crowninshield (the editor of *Vanity Fair,* another Nast publication) who were most helpful because "they thought I had talent." They were right.

"The photograph that I am most keenly proud of," Toni says, "is the one of a little boy sitting on a pile of rubble caused by the wanton V-2 bombing of London during the Second World War. I think I froze a moment there. I know I caught an emotion—that's what I'm after. I want to catch emotions and freeze them for all time like a rose in a cake of ice." The picture Frissell thinks of as her best was taken years after Agha and Crowninshield recognized her talent, but it has the qualities they divined in her earlier work—the ability to lock into an emotion, perhaps even anticipate it, waiting until it reaches full bloom in order to catch it at the precise second that it is released. By the time she was twenty-four, Frissell's own experience had given her ample opportunity to recognize tragedy when she saw it.

But her gift for recording emotion is not just limited to documenting tragedy; it is often just the opposite. She is by nature a strong, cheerful woman who adores the outdoors, thrives on skiing, fishing, shooting, and skin-diving; enjoys the company of men, loves and hates with passion and would rather photograph glee than gloom. She once told Winston Churchill during a sitting at Blenheim that though he might be the greatest thinker in the Western world he wasn't "thinking" the appropriate thoughts. "Mr. Churchill, are those the right thoughts for this moment? After all, I am trying to take your picture." She must have sounded like his American mother for the old warrior softened and the resulting portrait was by Lady Churchill's bed till the day she died. He must have liked it, too, for Frissell was asked

73

to return and photograph him in his ceremonial robes after Queen Elizabeth's coronation in 1953.

Two months before Roosevelt became President in 1932 Toni Frissell and Francis McNeil Bacon III were married. She was twenty-five years of age, a handsome woman who loved to drive cars that were always three or four sizes too small for her frame. As one old friend said, when she watched Toni emerge from a car, it looked as if she were unscrewing herself from the chassis. The Bacons settled down in St. James out on Long Island, and began to raise a family. First a boy named after Toni's brother, Varick, then a girl (Sidney Bacon Strafford) who has also become a photographer. Toni constantly photographed her children, which led her to use some of the work as illustrations for Robert Louis Stevenson's *A Child's Garden of Verses*. It was perhaps the kind of work she likes best—outside, unposed, and in natural light.

But the scenes for Stevenson's verses, documented in the pictures of beautiful children romping about an estate by Long Island Sound, cared for by the same governess who had tended Frissell when she was a girl, were not to last long. The war came and the f-stops that had caught the soft hazy world of St. James were closed down to the hard-edge events that were taking place in Europe and Asia. The old itch returned and the bucolic Long Island existence was traded in for adventure and excitement. Frissell packed her kit and left for England, first as official photographer for the Red Cross and then a second time on a special assignment for the Air Force. It was during the latter stint that she photographed the preflight briefing conducted by General Doolittle in which she captured the anxiety that played on the faces of the crews. There was a kind of resignation and meditative quality captured through the telltale betrayal of eye or lip that told everything there was to know about the bravery it took to climb into those B-24's and B-29's and head out over the Channel.

74

During the war Frissell traveled in Italy with the Allied troops. By the time she returned, she had pretty much decided that it was people and events she was going to focus on and that she would do less fashion photography. She did have an exclusive agreement with *Harper's Bazaar* from 1942 until 1952, as she had had with *Vogue* during the previous ten years, but in the 1950s she went over to *Sports Illustrated* and took on freelance assignments for *Life* and *Look*. By now she had earned a reputation that pretty much allowed her to pick and choose the commissions she wanted. Tame subjects took a back seat to any that had the edge of excitement. The need for adventure is not a male prerogative. There are many among the 300,000 photographs she took to prove it.

TONI
FRISSELL

1907   *Born Antoinette Montgomery Frissell, New York City*

1925   *Graduated from Miss Porter's School, Farmington, Connecticut*

1930   *Joined staff,* Vogue *magazine, as caption writer*

1931   *First experiments at fashion photography published in* Town and Country *magazine*

1931–1942   *Worked for* Vogue *as fashion photographer*

1932   *Married Francis McNeill Bacon III*

1933   *Son Varick born*

1935   *Daughter Sidney born*

1941   *Worked as official photographer for the Red Cross in England and Scotland*

1942   *Worked for* Harper's Bazaar

1944   *Toured Europe as guest photographer of the American 15th Air Force Squadron. Official photographer of the Women's Army Corps. Photographer for the Office of War Information*
Published illustrated version of Robert Louis Stevenson's A Child's Garden of Verses.

1946   *Published* The Happy Island, *based on a trip to Bermuda*

1947   *Award of distinctive merit for fashion photograph, "The Floating Boat," taken in Jamaica*

1953   *Invited to photograph Sir Winston Churchill. Began working for* Sports Illustrated

1955   *Participated in "The Family of Man" exhibition, Museum of Modern Art, New York*

1961   *Traveling exhibition, "A Number of Things through the Eyes of Toni Frissell," sponsored by the IBM Corporation*

1970   *Gave collection of negatives and prints to the Library of Congress*

1975   *Participated in traveling exhibition and book on the King Ranch, sponsored by the Amon Carter Museum. Permanent exhibit installed at King Ranch*

1975–1976   *Photographs in traveling exhibition, "Fashion Photogra-*

Frissell cover for Vogue, *July 1, 1941*

London, December 1942

Fashion shot for Vogue

Sherrewoque, the Bacon's 1689 house on Long Island

phy: Six Decades," *sponsored by the Emily Lowe Gallery, Hofstra University*

1977–1978 *Participated in traveling exhibition, "History of Fashion Photography," International Museum of Photography, George Eastman House*

Toni hanging flowers to dry

Tatyana Grosman

"SOMEHOW ONE HAS TO SAY GRACE"

"You know, I may be somebody who does not exist." When the visitor looks startled the tiny woman with a soft Russian accent goes on to explain. "Twice in my life I have been pronounced dead or nonexistent. The first time was when I was an infant in my father's house in Siberia and came down with a childhood disease, the name of which I don't even remember. The local doctor told my mother I would not recover. In Russia the custom was that after a child died the body was wrapped in towels and placed in a hot tub of herbal tea before burial. The doctor suggested to my mother that this ritual be advanced a few hours—a way of getting it behind her, I suppose. Well, I was placed in my burial broth, laid out to die, and by the next morning I was almost completely recovered. The bath had broken whatever it was I had."

The visitor asks her about the second experience. "It was forty years later, during the Second World War. My husband and I, with only the clothes on our backs and no papers, escaped into Spain from Occupied France. The American immigration official

79

Keith Brintzenhofe

in Barcelona, who was trying to get us entry permits to the States, turned to me and asked 'How can I make up papers for somebody who does not exist?.' Once again I had been pronounced dead."

Tatyana Grosman started out life in 1904 in the town of Ekaterinburg in the Ural Mountains as the daughter of Russian-Jewish intellectuals. She now lives in the village of Islip on Long Island, where she has a vital and necessary role in the New York art community when it comes to graphics. For Tatyana has earned a reputation as a lithographer that no one else approaches. Grosman thinks of a printing stone as a sacred object, which has a character or a flaw or a grain that helps make the image which is etched on it unique. To her, work is a dedication to her religion. She believes that "somehow one has to say grace."

There is a mysterious quality to this frail woman that is at once beguiling and intriguing. Like the lithographs she makes which are built up color on color, one stone for the red areas, another for the black and so on, each color making its own contribution and each affecting the others, her personality has been made up of many different layers of experience. The first layer is composed of her childhood which by all accounts was one of privilege. Her father, Semion Michailovitch Aguschewitsch, was a businessman who in addition to owning the Ekaterinburg newspaper, successfully speculated in real estate. Though her mother was of Russian descent, she had grown up in Bavaria and, never completely adjusting to the life in Ekaterinburg, would escape each summer with Tatyana and her younger brother to visit their grandparents in Munich. It was during the summer of 1914 while they were in Berchtesgaden that war broke out. "When the war began in August my family went to Switzerland, where the Russian consulate arranged for a number of us to travel back by ship across the Black Sea to Odessa, and by train back to the Urals." Because the Urals were far from the front lines, the war was not a particularly trying period for the Aguschewitsches. It would not be until after the October Revolution in 1917 when the Bolsheviks imprisoned Nicholas II and his family in Ekaterinburg that any real hardship was felt. They remained there for another year until the counterrevolutionary White Army under Admiral Alexander Vasilievich Kolchak seemed close to recapturing the town, which led to the execution of the Tsar and his family. Semion Michailovitch then fled with his family and one maid aboard the Trans-Siberian railroad to Vladivostok. Several months later, after continuing on to Japan, they settled in the European section of Yokohama. As she recalls, "My father was concerned about my education and sent me off to the Sacred Heart Convent in Tokyo where I learned to speak English by reading the Bible. I also learned about silence at Sacre Coeur where for three days out of each two weeks nobody was allowed to speak. The value of silence is better understood in the East than in the West."

Her father was concerned about other matters as well. On leaving Russia he, like many refugees, believed that it was only a temporary dislocation, but in time it became clear that they were never to return. Though he would have preferred to emigrate to America or to Switzerland, quota restrictions made it impossible so they returned to Germany and eventually settled in Dresden. For a young woman of seventeen years of age she had experienced much . . . in fact too much. Too many colors had been added too quickly; the previous ones had not been allowed to dry. It would take over two years for them to set: a period during which she took a vow of silence.

As the ink dried more colors were added. She tried music and then went to the Academy of Applied Arts in Dresden to study drawing with Professor Margaret Yunge, who "made me realize my potential." That is one of the reasons why today Mrs. Grosman likes working with younger artists, to help them realize theirs. But unquestionably the strongest color in her life was that of her husband, Maurice, with whom she spent some forty years until his death in 1967.

It was while at the Dresden academy that she met Grosman, who was studying at the Academy of Fine Arts. Up to then Tatyana seems to have been something of a model daughter, accompanying her mother to the mountains in the winter, resorts on the North Sea or in Italy in the summer, and to spas and the capitals of Europe in between. Maurice Grosman, on the other hand, was a struggling, penniless young artist from Poland. Her parents were not thrilled with the relationship. "Probably the most painful decision of my life was to break with my parents," she is reported to have said. "I became seriously ill and spent two months in the hospital."

Tatyana has a gossamer-like voice rich with intonations which reflect her mood and create for the listener a sense of pathos or pleasure depending upon the events recalled. When she speaks of the eight years before the war when she and Maurice lived in Montparnasse, there is an exuberant chime of happiness, and it is said that when she mentions her daughter Larissa, who died at sixteen months, her voice becomes as hollow as a gong. But for the most part the voice chimes when she talks of the bohemian life they led in Paris and the long summers spent at Céret, an artist's colony in the Pyrenees, where Maurice painted and she read poetry. "We were young, poor, and very much in love." Then came the Occupation of France when all painting and poetry gave way to sheer survival.

As Tatyana described their escape from France I began to wonder if in fact I was not in the presence of a holy woman: a woman made holy by having been the subject of not one but a whole series of miracles. She and Maurice slipped out of Paris two days before the Occupation and made their way south to Céret, where they remained for a year. In 1941 they moved on to Marseilles in hopes of obtaining a visa to the United States. But instead Maurice was rounded up with several thousand other Jews and placed in a detention center at Alzon, a village above Nîmes, where she was allowed to join him. In time a message arrived from the American consul in Marseilles stating that their visa had been approved but must be exercised within fourteen days. It also said that a document would have to be signed by an official in every town between Alzon and Marseilles in addition to which they must obtain proof from the Paris police that neither of them had ever been convicted of a crime.

While Tatyana managed to obtain the necessary signatures from the officials between Alzon and Marseilles, by going to each of them herself, her clearance from Paris did not come through in time. They did discover, however, that an extension might be obtained if Maurice could prove he was hospitalized and so, after a frantic search for admission into a hospital, they found a private sanatorium where he was accepted. Tatyana returned to her small hotel room to await results. She didn't have to wait long for one night the police came by with orders to arrest all Jews. Leaving by the nearest window she hid behind a chimney until they had left. Returning to her room she discovered that the police were making a second sweep so this time she fled for good, leaving all her possessions.

For the next two weeks she hid in the sanatorium with Maurice each night until the police came there, too, in search of Jews. Barely escaping, they eventually made their way to a village named Le Boulou near the Spanish border where they lived for a few weeks until given directions by a local resident on how to cross into Spain. One day at high noon they strolled out of Le Boulou carrying as a decoy Maurice's painting material. Of other possessions they were bereft. They spent the night in the forest and the following morning saw a young shepherd ("perhaps nineteen years of age") on a ledge nearby praying. The shepherd rose and beckoned them to follow. He then led them with his flock across the border and into Spain. They passed the first night at his farm. The next morning the boy blessed them and returned with his flock to the mountains. For the next three weeks ("I wish it had never ended") they walked through Spain, first following

83

the La Mouga River and then by other routes, but avoiding the main roads for fear of being caught, until they reached Barcelona, where once again Tatyana became, for the American immigration official, "somebody who does not exist." Fortunately, the Hebrew Immigrant Aid Society took a different view and obtained visas for them to enter the United States in 1943.

When the Grosmans first arrived they lived in a small apartment on Eighth Street in the Village. Maurice taught painting, supplemented their income by selling his own work, and began silk-screen modern paintings that he sold through Marlboro bookshops. In 1955 he suffered a heart attack, after which they moved to a small house, purchased some years before, in Islip. It was in this house that Tatyana would begin her work as a lithographer through the most bizarre series of events. As she tells it, in order to earn a living, she took over from Maurice his silk screening of original paintings. In time her reproductions came to the attention of Bill Liberman, then at the Museum of Modern Art, who though much impressed with their quality, was barred from buying any for the museum because they were considered reproductions rather than originals—the distinction being that the artist who made the drawings had done so on paper rather than directly on the silk screen itself. While it is possible to work directly on silk screens and create originals, Tatyana was not fond of the process. She "didn't like the smell." But lithography was a process which she did admire. As she has said, "Through some miracle there turned up in our yard two lithographic limestones—not just any old lithographic stone, but two from Bavaria which are considered to be the finest available. They came from a quarry no longer in use. Some weeks later I discovered that neighbors had a lithographic press that they were willing to sell for fifteen dollars . . . it was all very mysterious." For the art world it was also all very fortunate.

Lithography, or writing on stone, was first discovered by Aloys Senefelder in Munich about 1798 and is based on the mutual antipathy of water and oil. The artist sketches his design on a porous limestone with a special crayon or a greasy substance known as tuche, after which the entire surface is dampened with a combination of gum arabic and water. Only the blank areas absorb the water mixture; the greasy design areas repel it. Ink made of soap, wax, oil, and lampblack is then rolled on, which coats the greasy area but is rejected by the moist part. A clean reverse impression of the design is made when a sheet of paper is pressed against the stone. With subsequent inkings any number of impressions may be made until the stone is worn out and in theory any number of stones may be employed, permitting the artist a wide range of colors.

Whether she knows it or not, it is clear that Tatyana Grosman, in her attempts at music and painting, in her love of poetry, her choice of a husband, and selection of friends, has always had the nature of an artist. The reason she herself did not grasp the fact was perhaps that she did not find her means of expression until she began practicing lithography—but other artists recognized a kindred spirit. Artists have a foxhound's nose for picking up that scent. The foxhounds in this case were Larry Rivers and Frank O'Hara, who commissioned Tatyana to print a book at her newly formed Universal Limited Art Edition, which was to become a classic. The book contained Rivers's drawings and O'Hara's poetry and, symbolically enough, was entitled *Stone.* It did not make the best-seller lists; it wasn't supposed to, having been limited to an edition of twenty-five of which the Museum of Modern Art bought a number. What it did do was bring together the work of two highly sensitive artists, reproduced by another artist, for the enjoyment of a very limited audience.

It was an experiment all around, for back in 1959 when the book was published artists were not thinking about working in lithography. In the first place there were almost no good lithographers to work with. But Mrs. Grosman changed all that, so today Jasper Johns, Robert Motherwell, Barnett Newman, Jim Dine,

Alexander Liberman, Roy Lichtenstein, and a legion of others visit her modest house to work with the lady's stones. They come because they recognize the artist in her. They know she is a great printer and I suspect they smell a saint. For saints are made for giving, and their good works remain after them. This is and will be surely true of Tatyana Grosman, for she has built her house on stone.

Young Tatyana in Russia

1924, with parents and brother Victor

TATYANA
GROSMAN

With Maruice, West Islip, New York

With Jasper Johns

(*Left to right*) *Robert Rauschenberg, Tatyana Grosman, Bill Goldston, Frank Akers, Zigmund Priede, Marion Javits*

1904 Born Tatyana Aguschewitsch in Ekaterinburg, in the Ural Mountains, Russia

1912 Graduated from the Gymnasium

1919 Left Russia and traveled to Japan with her family

1920 Attended Convent of the Sacred Heart, Tokyo

1921 Traveled with her family to Italy and then to Germany. Studied at the Academy of Applied Arts, Dresden

1931 Married Maurice Grosman in Berlin

1931–1940 Lived in Paris on Montparnasse

1940–1943 Lived in southern France and Barcelona, Spain

1943 Moved to New York

1950 Became a United States citizen

1956 Founded Universal Limited Art Editions in West Islip, New York

1959 Met Larry Rivers and Frank O'Hara. Published Stone

1967 Maurice Grosman died

1982 Died, July 24

Phyllis Ann Harrison-Ross

"POVERTY PRODUCES STRESS AND STRESS PRODUCES ILLNESS"

In his collected work, *Talks to Teachers,* William James made the observation, "Man, whatever else he may be, is primarily a practical being whose mind is given him to aid in adapting him to this world's life." He made these remarks back in 1892 or thereabouts, in one of a series of addresses at Harvard on the psychology of teaching. Though James resided in an orderly world and associated with genteel people who lived a life of the mind and were trained to be responsive to duty, aware of mission, and conscious of manners, his theory applies equally well to the less privileged. It is, in fact, being put to the acid test right now in the slums of Spanish Harlem on the East Side of Manhattan.

Dr. Harrison-Ross, who practices psychiatry in Spanish Harlem, spends each day dealing with the effects of this particular world on the people who live in it. "Poverty," she says, "is probably one of the major causes of disorders in children. Living in poverty and seeing the things that poverty produces in a community, having parents who are disillusioned and disappointed and angry and unskilled, whose needs are not met, is probably the

91

number-one cause of mental problems per se, whether it shows up in mental illness or learning disabilities or mental retardation or alcoholism or problems of child abuse. I think one of the worst things that can happen to a person is to be born poor."

Dr. Harrison-Ross remembers her own childhood as "a good childhood with wonderfully attentive parents. . . . We weren't rich, but I had the kind of attention that I think children should have." Her father was a school superintendent in the public school system of Detroit. Her mother, early in her career, was a social worker and later a professor of social work at Wayne State University. She says her parents "pushed me toward law or the medical profession. I think I can remember as far back as the age of four deciding that I was going to be a doctor, and I've never really waivered from that." But she also recognized the realities of being a black woman in this country and the fact that, as her parents kept telling her, "You are going to have to take care of yourself and make something of yourself because the odds are against you."

Phyllis Harrison (she added the name Ross when she married Ed Ross) first became aware of the odds when she was about five years old and her mother and father moved from the white neighborhood in which they had been living to a black section of Detroit. The tale she tells is a metaphor for how prejudice creates a no-win situation for all involved. Pointing to the pictures on her office wall, she says, "As you can see, my mother looks as though she were white, and while my maternal grandmother was white, her husband was black, as was my father and all his forebears. Early on we lived with my maternal grandmother when my parents were first married and finishing college. My mother's brother also lived there with his white wife and their four children. We had a happy, close family life, not only in the big house in Detroit, but up on Grandma's farm during the summer as well. Then, at the point when I began to attend public school my father said, 'This relationship cannot continue—each branch of the family must go its separate way.'

"You see," she explains, "my cousins could not really survive and admit that they were partly black, looking the way they did and deciding to be white, and that meant they couldn't afford to have relatives around who were obviously black; that was the reality of the situation. And so they moved into their own home in a white neighborhood, and we moved into a black one and . . . I missed them." (It is only in recent years that Dr. Harrison-Ross and her cousins have been in contact, but they obviously kept track of her growing reputation in medicine, because when one of them developed an aneurysm of the arteries in his brain and was advised to have surgery, it was she whom he called to solicit an opinion on the wisdom of such a move and to seek advice on the best possible people to perform the operation.)

While some things obviously changed in her life when she moved away from the cousins, others, such as the push she got from her parents, remained constant. Dr. Harrison-Ross speaks with some reverence when she says, "They were very successful and substantial people, supportive and encouraging and their influence really impacted upon me. The black side of my family had for three generations back gone to college—my paternal great-grandfather having graduated from Oberlin, his daughter from Spelman, and my father from Morehouse and the University of Michigan. Some psychologists maintain that 'imitation shades imperceptibly into emulation . . . and emulation is the very nerve center of human society.' " That she graduated from Albion College at twenty, and from Wayne State University College of Medicine at twenty-three, indicates that the intensity of her character had something to do, not only with her parents' "push," but with her emulation of their drive.

Asked if she was discriminated against in medical school, Phyllis Harrison-Ross is quick to say no. "I think that being a woman

. . . if anything, I got special attention. I very rarely ran up against racial discrimination, but there was sex discrimination. The only problem was the question of fraternities, which were segregated and naturally, being a woman and being black, I couldn't belong. Of course, it was at the fraternities where one could study past medical exams and get advice from the older students . . . but to compensate for being excluded from fraternities, several of us formed a study group. . . . It worked out pretty well."

One gets the impression that here is a person who will always manage to work things out. Another impression the visitor gets is that she likes people. As one of her friends has said, "Phyllis would make a damned good politician." The chief reason she switched from pediatrics, for which she was trained at Wayne State, to the practice of psychiatry, is that her outgoing personality requires the feeding of friendships. "I really enjoy talking with patients," she says, "but in pediatrics you have to see a very large number and you really can't afford the time to sit and talk with them. So I went into psychiatry."

In her small spartan office on 98th Street and Second Avenue in Manhattan she sits in a swivel chair before an oak elbow-shaped desk surrounded by pictures of her favorite sport—scuba diving—and looks very much like a model for Gaston Lachaise, radiating the same healthy confidence and self-reliance that he captured in his sculpture of strong women. She appears to be a woman with a cool mentality and a warm soul, for she conveys the dual quality of one who does not suffer fools gladly, but who would be comforting to anyone (including fools) in moments of stress or panic—the kind of person you would want on your side in times of crisis. In fact she spends much of her time in crisis situations and with people under stress because as she says, "poverty produces stress and stress produces illness."

In order that I might see at firsthand the kind of work Dr. Harrison-Ross and her staff are doing, she turned me over to Dolores Leviant, one of her psychotherapists who works with emotionally disturbed children and their parents, and who sees every day the results that stress inflicts on families. Children up to five years of age are brought in to be treated for phobias that range from an inability to speak or a refusal to eat, to the dread of walking downstairs or just a plain fear of living. One form of therapy designed to help children gradually overcome a speaking block consists of arranging the five to ten parents and children in a circle on small chairs and having a group-sing. This, together with other forms of therapy, including water-play, painting, and the manipulation of puppets, are part of the curriculum.

One of the problems that black and Hispanic mothers—or any working mothers—have to face is what to do with the children while away at work. Harrison-Ross is in agreement with Kenneth Keniston, the sociologist, who argues that "work, not the families, should be reshaped to fit the needs of the families." Keniston wrote in *An American Anachronism: The Image of Women and Work:* "It should no longer be assumed that families are not the business of employers or public officials." As Harrison-Ross says, "In Sweden there are over one hundred thousand day-care centers which care for preschool children when the parents are at work." She also knows that in Sweden they have other innovative programs, such as the three-family system in which an individual is hired to care for the children of three working or student families in the children's own homes. The children remain at home— going to one another's houses on a rotating basis—a formula designed to maintain a sense of security through the child's familiarity with his surroundings. The fees parents pay amount to only a fraction of the total cost, the rest being financed through government or municipal funds.

In many cases the best the black working mother in this country can hope for is to have good neighbors who will look out for her children. "Of course," Harrison-Ross adds, "many black mothers still work as domestics who have to get to somebody's house in time to prepare the breakfast, and they don't leave until after the dinner dishes are done. These women manage to find twenty minutes a day to spend with their children and that amount of time I believe can do for a kid. Of course, the children themselves grow up at a very young age, but they are made to recognize the reality of the situation."

Dr. Harrison-Ross has pioneered in the rehabilitation of children who were considered hopelessly retarded, emotionally disturbed, or physically disabled. At the Rose F. Kennedy Center for Research in Mental Retardation and Human Development, where she was Psychiatric Director between 1966 and 1972, Phyllis helped to develop beginning programs in physical and mental therapy for the young. "There simply weren't any school programs for the disturbed child, and so they just stayed at home. We designed special programs and developed models which were duplicated in the public school so that these children could have a learning environment. We concentrated on helping them develop their self-awareness, and to learn to love themselves and other people, which was not easy for them. As instructors, we used hippies, former dropouts, and a variety of unusual, skilled teachers to work with them."

One of the methods of reeducation that the doctor is firmly against is the use of corporal punishment in the name of discipline. She served on a committee to investigate corporal punishment in a New York City junior high school and became bothered by its widespread use.

A phrase that Dr. Harrison-Ross often uses in describing both her life and her evaluation of events and circumstances is "the reality of the situation." This way of looking at things may go back to the time when her father saw that each branch of the family should go its separate way. But being an activist, she does more than simply recognize realities—she acts on them. Recognizing that families are the business of employers and public officials, she is working to establish a day-care center where children of staff members may be left when there is no one at home

to watch them. She is working on a "drop-in" recreation area—
for parents to leave their children when coming to the hospital
for treatment and which she hopes will someday lead to a health-
education center with literature, pamphlets, and other learning
aids so children can begin to understand some of the rudiments
of a healthy survival. "They may prefer to use their neighbors,
friends, or others . . . that's up to them, but the options should
be there."

For Dr. Harrison-Ross there are, of course, other "realities,"
such as work in the New York prison system, in her capacity as
forensic psychiatrist to the Medical Review Board of New York
State, which is charged with investigating all deaths that occur in
jails; the development of medical hygieine services for the under-
served members of our population (Asian-Americans, Pacific Is-
landers, Hispanics, and Alaskan natives); and the question of
alcoholism and drug abuse, which she must address in her work
as a member of an advisory committee to the Secretary of the U.S.
Department of Health. And so it goes . . . the realities of the
situation are endless. She has written at considerable length on
these subjects in her psychological textbooks for junior and senior high school students, entitled *Getting It Together, The Black
Child, Understanding Parenthood,* as well as for other specialized
publications.

Given the realities of Dr. Harrison-Ross' crowded professional
life, it is a wonder that she ever found time to marry. In fact, when
she did find a man to whom she was attracted, her work got in
the way. As she describes it, "I met my future husband at the
altar. Some mutual friends were getting married and had asked
us to stand up with them. He seemed to have a lot of qualities that
I admired and had always wanted in a man. I was twenty-eight or
twenty-nine then, sure I wasn't going to find anyone good
enough, and then all of a sudden there he was. I found him
attractive. That night he walked me home and asked when could
he see me again. 'In three months,' I said. It was absolutely

97

unconscious . . . it just popped out. Well, he called me the next day because he is a lawyer and lawyers don't give up easily, and by that time I had it together and so we started going out." They were married in 1970.

Though the people in Spanish Harlem may have more than their fair share of problems, they are fortunate to have Dr. Phyllis Ann Harrison-Ross in their midst . . . and that's the reality of that situation.

PHYLLIS ANN HARRISON-ROSS

Phyllis Ann at eleven

1936   Born Phyllis Ann Harrison in Detroit, Michigan

1956   B.A., Albion College

1959   M.D., Wayne State University College of Medicine

1959–1960   Internship, rotating, Kings County Hospital, Brooklyn

1961–1962   Instructor of Pediatrics at Cornell Medical School

1960–1962   Residency, New York Hospital, Cornell Medical School

1962–1964   Residency, Albert Einstein College of Medicine, Bronx Municipal Hospital Center

1964–1966   Adult Psychiatry—Fellowship: Albert Einstein College of Medicine, Bronx Municipal Hospital Center

1965–1972   Consultant to Head Start

1966–1968   Instructor of Pediatrics and Psychology, Albert Einstein College of Medicine

1968–1972   Assistant Professor of Pediatrics and Psychiatry, Albert Einstein College of Medicine

1970   Married Edward Ross

1970–1973   Member of President's National Advisory Council on Drug Abuse Prevention

1972   Professor of Clinical Psychiatry, New York Medical College

1976   Member of Medical Review Board, New York State Commission of Corrections

1977   Member of New York State Alcoholism Advisory Committee

1978   Member of Minority Advisory Committee to the Secretary of the U.S. Department of Health, Education and Welfare

1979   Chairman of Advisory Council of Minority Affairs, New York State Office of Mental Health

Vith her parents at her mother's graduation   Family portraits in Harrison-Ross' office

Virginia Johnson-Masters

"SEXUAL DISORDERS ARE FAMILY CONCERNS"

One of the reasons Mrs. Johnson-Masters doesn't satisfy the image of someone likely to proselytize on controversial subjects, and one of the reasons both she and her husband, Dr. William Masters, have been so successful, is that they both genuinely personify all those wholesome qualities that are the woof and warp of their heritage and upbringing.

The background of this soft-spoken, hazel-eyed woman is about as American as it is possible to be. Her paternal grandmother's family, who came from Virginia, were among the three founding families of Springfield, Missouri, while her paternal grandfather's family, the Eshelmans, helped settle, back in the early eighteenth century, Germantown, Pennsylvania. On her mother's side, her forebears were hill people from Appalachia while her maternal grandfather was a Southern gentleman from Alabama. Though her people were not revolutionaries, they were pioneers, so it is not surprising that Mrs. Johnson-Masters, who is herself very much of a pioneer, was willing to accept Dr. Mas-

103

Scott F. Johnson

ters's offer back in 1957 to become his assistant in sex research
—a controversial subject at the time.

Since childhood Johnson had wanted only to pursue a career
in music, having started out at fourteen (during her last two years
at the Golden City High School in Lamar, Missouri) studying
voice at nearby Drury College, after which she went on to take
private voice lessons. As she says, "Music is the only thing I ever
really wanted to do. . . . I would, given the choice, rather be a
member of a glorious chorus without even the identity of a soloist
. . . than do anything else in the world. It's the only thing that I
can truly identify with as representing my point of view . . . my
outlook on life." When she says this there is a rather lonely sound
in her voice as if she had lost someone dear that she will never
see again. Though it does not appear that she has lost something,
but rather that it was denied her.

Johnson's mother is reported to have been a very overbearing
woman. On the one hand the child was treated like a "little doll"
and given everything that she could conceivably want, while on
the other she was denied the only thing she really wanted, which
was to become a singer, because her mother did not consider it
a worthy career. "Why not become a teacher as I did?" she would
be asked. Whether it is a question of worthiness or jealousy will
remain obscure for she remembers the time when she was singing
with her mother in a farm club grange meeting, and hitting a high
note that her mother could not reach and being told, "Don't you
sing those high notes, they're too high for you."

"I was so intimidated that I couldn't sing above my bridge for
two years without literally choking on it."

On the other hand, she recalls a time when she was twelve
years of age and performing at her grade school graduation when
her mother, who was expecting a baby that same day, refused to
go to the hospital until her daughter had performed, so the
question arose as to who was going to deliver what first in the
auditorium of ol' Golden City grammar school. Fortunately, Vir-

ginia's performance took place first, allowing her mother time to drive to the hospital seventeen miles away where a baby brother was born some three hours later. Mrs. Eshelman's ambiguous behavior would plague her daughter for the next twenty years until she met Dr. Masters and settled into the Masters-Johnson partnership which made both of them famous.

Virginia Johnson-Masters is a woman who radiates goodwill and a straight-from-the-shoulder openness that is beguiling. Dressed in a white doctor's smock, her Prince Valiant haircut falling on her collar and bangs curtaining her forehead, she recites the events of her early life as if she were one of her patients filling out a questionnaire. The answers must be accurate—no facts omitted and above all they must be honest. "Up to the time I went to the University of Missouri I was a very protected child, so when I got to college—that heavenly world of everything—I tried to learn everything immediately. I took courses in psychology, the theory of music, economics—you name it. The result was that I became overwhelmed, contracted pneumonia and ran away to Kansas City. The only thing I was sure of is that I was not going to return to a home environment. Before attending the university I had broken off an engagement to a lawyer who was twice my age, and when I returned to Kansas City I reconstructed the romance simply to keep from going back home. I was so lonely and there was not one single person who knew that I needed help." You ask Mrs. Johnson-Masters a question and you get an answer. It is probably this openness which helps her own patients discuss such intimate problems as sexual incompatability.

It was with her first husband that she went to St. Louis and took a job on a court newspaper called the *Daily Record.* Having married an attorney she felt taking a job that was connected with the law was somehow expected of her, and "I have always been a great helper of people who wanted help." The marriage lasted about a year, the job about three, and although she was urged to remain on the *Record* and become its treasurer, she chose to join in the advertising department of radio station KWOJ in the vain hope that some opportunity to sing might arise. "I went there because I wanted to sing, and it was just a way of getting inside. By the time I was there a year I knew everybody in the CBS hierarchy, but it was a nothing life. . . . I had been inoculated by my mother with a lot of initiative that did not carry with it the drive to make things happen." It was about this time that she met George Johnson, "an incredibly talented musician and Peter Pan" whom she married and with whom she had two children. Her analysis of their marriage leaves little doubt that Johnson-Masters demands from herself the same candid appraisal of her past that she would of any patient who came for help. "It was a very interesting and very pleasant marriage until the children came. I was a singer, sang with George's band, but after Scott and Lisa were born I had to stop being a night person and take care of them. He was never able to make the adjustment, so we divorced. . . . He was a charming man." After the divorce she went to Washington University with the idea of getting into a degree program in sociology, but with two children she couldn't afford that, so she ended up taking a job at the Washington University School of Medicine. It was here that she met Bill Masters.

William Howard Masters II had become interested in the subject of sex research in his third year at the University of Rochester's School of Medicine and set out to make a contribution to the then almost nonexistent store of knowledge having to do with the physiology of sex. Masters was fortunate in having as a teacher the late Dr. George Washington Corner who, even before Dr. Alfred Kinsey, was amassing scientific data on human sexuality. Corner advised Masters to wait until he was more mature, had earned a reputation in some other field, and secured the support of a prestigious medical school. And this was exactly the program that Masters followed. In 1954, at the age of thirty-eight, after having become a distinguished professor and researcher in the field of obstetrics and gynecology, he was given approval to conduct sex research under the auspices of the Washington University School of Medicine in St. Louis.

Though Kinsey's report had taken the first steps, Masters wanted to observe, measure, and record what was happening physiologically while sexual activity was taking place. Little was known, for example, about the physiology of the orgasm or if sexual cycles were different in men and women, or if sex problems in marriage were widespread or even if the male superior position was most satisfying and natural. (The answer to the latter, according to Masters and Johnson, is not necessarily, so it depends on your preference, not to mention physical and anatomical considerations.) In any case, Masters began by interviewing prostitutes (27 male and 118 female) in an attempt to establish a methodology and, although he admits to having learned a great deal from them, he never did include any of his findings in the statistics he compiled and the reports he published. They were simply too migratory and hard to keep track of, as well as not being typical in that it was difficult to find a prostitute with a normal, uncongested pelvic region and organ not distended from overuse. There was, however, one unusually intelligent and intuitive prostitute who had earned a Ph.D. in sociology, but lately given up the study of the function of human groups to concentrate on men, one at a time, because she apparently found that was more rewarding than group therapy. While Masters had earlier begun to recognize his need for a female partner, it seems to have been a dialogue with this prostitute that clarified his thinking and established his resolve. The story is that this fallen sociologist made periodic trips to St. Louis to see Dr. Masters for a gynecological checkup and during one of her visits she broached the question as to whether or not it wouldn't be useful to have a woman assistant because, she told him, he would never understand what had to be known about the psychosocial aspects of female sexuality without a female collaborator to act as his interpreter. As Mrs. Johnson-Masters says, "This rather put into words what Bill had been thinking about for some time but never really come down on. She helped him to understand that you simply cannot put yourself in the skin of another sex."

When Masters finally started looking for a female assistant he did not specify an M.D. or a health professional among the qualifications. He did demand an ability to relate to other people, being between twenty-five and thirty years of age, married or previously married, and having borne at least one child so that the candidate had experienced an intimate relationship as well as being familiar with childbirth and motherhood. Mrs. Johnson says that the reason Masters didn't look for an M.D. was that "he is very canny and probably wouldn't have gotten an M.D." The whole subject was so controversial that a woman doctor stood a real chance of jeopardizing her career by agreeing to such a collaboration. Also, the collaboration was to be a long one (in their case it became lifelong) because he had set out to establish a base of physiological knowledge about which nothing was then known. He set out to do this in order to be of real help to sexually troubled people, as opposed to just gathering data.

The collaboration began in 1957, and as Virginia says, "I was very much the student for about two years and in spite of my lack of initiative I gradually worked myself in because once I'm on track I let very little stand in my way. I started out as an employee and wound up as a kind of second partner," she added with some modesty. "I didn't have an M.D., I didn't have a medical education, and I was nondegreed, as a matter of fact. Overeducated and nondegreed." In 1971 she married Bill Masters and together they have written six books, observed 1,076 volunteers perform every conceivable sexual act, analyzed over 14,000 orgasms, and treated in excess of 3,500 couples for sexual dysfunctions.

In moving away from prostitutes, to just "plain folks" as they refer to them, they were able to establish a body of knowledge over the next eleven years that included studies on 380 females and 312 male volunteers who had been subjected to a variety of positions and techniques in order to analyze if and how sexual response differed from individual to individual and between the sexes. Couples who volunteered for various reasons—because they had a problem of their own, or wanted to contribute to science, or just to indulge in permissive sex—were interviewed in depth. An ability to articulate their own subjective feelings after having sex was important; objective determinations were left to the researchers. If the volunteers passed the interview (and it has been reported that many did not), they were assigned to a small soundproof room and told of the particular activity the doctor wanted to monitor. The door was closed and they were left alone. Later, when the couple became familiar with the environment, the door would be left ajar, and Masters and Johnson would work in an adjoining room assuring the couple that they would not be observed. Next, they were told that on occasion a researcher might pass through the room, but to continue with their activities, and finally, the observations and documentary filming would take place. Sometimes, they would bring in physiologists who would monitor them on an EKG machine or measure their blood pressure or they would introduce some special equipment such as soft water-filled tampons, or with their female subjects, an artificial penis designed by radiophysicists with which they masturbated in order to record changes going on inside the vagina and determine the effectiveness of varying contraceptives or to help create "artificial vaginas" in women who needed them.

Though the research they developed was to help sexually troubled people, their methods seemed shocking and created controversy. For most of us who learned about sex in the locker room before Masters and Johnson introduced it into the classroom, it was hard to accept that this censored and very private subject had now gone public and was being observed in the laboratory and recorded as statistical information. The critic Albert Goldman, while reviewing *Human Sexual Response,* was particularly offended by the artificial penis which his review in *Book World* referred to as the "plastic dildo." Goldman wrote: "Perhaps a genuinely prophetic imagination is declaring itself in the book's most indelible image, that of a woman mating with herself by means of a machine." The psychiatrist Natalie Shaines accused Masters and Johnson of debasing sex. In 1966 when *HSR* was published, psychiatrists were, for the most part, suspicious about the team's claim to be able to cure most sexual dysfunctions through short-term treatment because they still accepted the Freudian concept that all sexual problems arose from deep unconscious conflicts. But they had their defenders, too. Dr. Sager, also a pioneer in couple therapy, observed that their real contribution was the treatment of the relationship rather than the individual. As Mrs. Johnson puts it herself, "Sexual disorders are family concerns. . . . If something is going wrong, it is going wrong between two people and then it becomes the relationship which is the medium of the psychotherapy." Bill Masters put it another way. "The heart had been measured with mechanical equipment for years, and so have the eyes, and the stomach, and the whatnot, but as soon as the subject is sex, however . . . " A shake of the head finishes the sentence.

Human Sexual Response documents what happens to the body while a couple is making love. Before they published their findings on the physiology of a body, the sexual-response cycle was observed 10,000 times as it proceeded from excitement to plateau to orgasm and finally to resolution.

Though written in what *Playboy* describes as Latinate Medicalese, *HSR* became a best seller, and its findings have never been challenged. Their second book, *Human Sexual Inadequacy*, which describes their treatment method, came out four years later in 1970 and was written primarily for the family physician whose medical training they found was, almost without exception, insufficient in dealing with what they termed "sexual incompatibility." Masters and Johnson believed that the family physician was in a key position to offer advice to distressed couples. Apart from the family physician, the male gynecologists were woefully ignorant of female feelings about their bodies, about sexuality, and about pregnancy. Mrs. Johnson-Master's soapbox remark was "Give me a male gynecologist, and I'll show you someone who doesn't know anything about women." As Dr. Masters told the American Medical Association in 1972, the medical profession is not prepared by their training "to accept sex as a natural function," the inference being that you cannot solve a problem if you don't recognize its existence.

One of the problems Masters and Johnson set out to solve was the question of treatment for sexual dysfunctions by physiological methods, even though they recognized that most problems of inadequacy were psychologically oriented. However, psychotherapy had so often proved inadequate they wanted to develop a short-term psychological treatment which, when refined, would in most cases be able to complete the cure in about two weeks. Their research indicated that the primary problem with couples suffering dysfunctions was generated by ignorance and apprehension about their sexual performance. Their cure was to prescribe a form of direct learning about their bodies and how they react to various forms of touching. After the initial sexual histories were taken, the patients were encouraged to experiment as to which type of touching felt good. They developed what they termed "sensate focus," encouraging couples to discover the pleasures of touching each other and graduating through a hierarchy of "tasks" with nongenital touching first, then genital touching, and finally intercourse. They reported about a 20 percent failure rate with the treatment.

One of the points that Mrs. Johnson-Masters keeps stressing is the difference between the work they were doing up to 1970 and the work they have been performing since. Until 1970 they worked with a "research population" establishing a base of physiological knowledge, and since then they have been involved in purely clinical research attempting—and with great success it is said—to help couples with problems related to sexual inadequacy, incompatibility, and other related difficulties. Indeed, among their contributions, they made communication about sex possible and acceptable, thus tearing down one of the barriers that made any cure so much more difficult. Writing in the publication *Sexual Medicine Today* Harry Henderson made the point that Masters and Johnson made communication about sexuality legitimate. "It is clear that *after* Masters and Johnson is markedly different than *before* and that they are among the leading scientific heroes of our age in alleviating the anguish accompanying sexual dysfunctions."

VIRGINIA
JOHNSON-MASTERS

Johnson in her laboratory

1925 Born Virginia Eshelman, Springfield, Missouri
1940–1942 Drury College, Springfield, Missouri
1944–1946 Missouri University, Columbia, Missouri
1947–1950 Editorial writer and administrative secretary, St. Louis Daily Record
1950 Married George Johnson
1950–1951 Advertising Department, Columbia Broadcasting System (KMOX)(KWOJ), St. Louis
1952 Son Scott Forstall born
1955 Daughter Lisa Evans born
1956 Divorced George Johnson
1957–1964 Research Staff, Washington University School of Medicine, Division of Reproductive Biology, Department of Obstetrics and Gynecology, St. Louis. Worked with William H. Masters
1962–1964 Research Instructor, Washington School of Medicine, Division of Reproductive Biology, Department of Obstetrics and Gynecology, St. Louis
1964–1969 Research Associate, Reproductive Biology Research Foundation, St. Louis
1966 Published, with William H. Masters, Human Sexual Response
1970 Published, with William H. Masters, Human Sexual Inadequacy
1971 Married William H. Masters
1969–1973 Assistant Director, Reproductive Biology Research Foundation, St. Louis
1973–1980 Co-Director (with William H. Masters), Masters & Johnson Institute, (formerly Reproductive Biology Research Foundation), St. Louis
1981–present Director, Masters & Johnson Institute, St. Louis

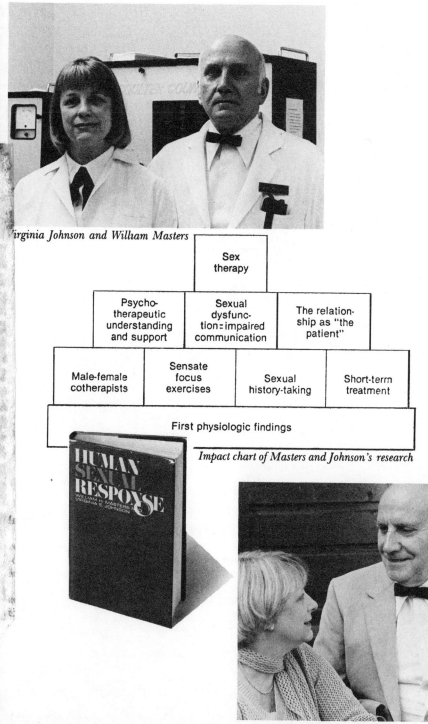

Virginia Johnson and William Masters

| Sex therapy |
| Psycho-therapeutic understanding and support | Sexual dysfunc-tion = impaired communication | The relation-ship as "the patient" |
| Male-female cotherapists | Sensate focus exercises | Sexual history-taking | Short-term treatment |
| First physiologic findings |

Impact chart of Masters and Johnson's research

HUMAN SEXUAL RESPONSE
WILLIAM H. MASTERS, M.D.
VIRGINIA E. JOHNSON

Johnson and Masters, 1981

Elsa Leichter

"FAMILIES ARE MY RAW MATERIAL"

Most of the people who come to Elsa Leichter seeking advice on family problems are there because of difficulty with a child. For more than forty years now, this delicate, blue-eyed woman, who looks as if she has stepped out of a Renoir pastel, has been the director of the group therapy program for the Jewish Family Services in New York City, counseling parents and their children on how to cope with problems, real or imagined. "The problems that come to my attention range from children who are predelinquents, presenting behavioral problems, or who do not achieve their potential in school, have neurotic difficulties, or who simply have the habit of running away."

Even though Elsa Leichter herself had a fairly happy childhood, she, too, once left home when she was a little girl of seven. But in her case she was not so much running away as running toward something—the foothills of the Alps which lay beyond the outskirts of her native Vienna. "The mountains looked so close, but after an hour or so I got lost, and I started crying and was brought home by the police. When I was a bit older, our class would go to the Vienna Woods on outings. . . . I remember being immensely excited by the smell of the pine forest, the cow dung, the damp earth, and all that is deliciously foreign to a city child." Seventy-five years later, the mountains still hold the same attraction for her. She loves to walk in them alone, and yet she admits she is not athletic. When she was a child, it was hard for her to keep pace with her companions, and she "always had to fight to keep up." But then, she has been a natural-born fighter all her life.

Good fighters do not come from soft backgrounds and Elsa Leichter is a case in point. Her parents were Jewish immigrants from Eastern Europe, and she remembers that when she was a child they were very poor. Her father, Emil Schweiger, meaning "the silent one," was totally self-educated, but he nevertheless instilled in his three daughters an enjoyment of culture by telling them stories of the theater and singing arias from the operas he loved so much. He insisted that Elsa study Latin and Greek, and when she had finished preparatory school she enrolled in a pre-med course at the university. Emil's daughter would have a profession and not have to rely as he did on the vagaries of a small shop for survival. Elsa left the university after the pre-med course, which she admits "was not the story of wisdom." It may have been the story of self-sacrifice, because she could not stand the idea of her mother going without the things she needed so that Elsa could become a doctor. Elsa admits that there is another side of the story, though. She was having a romance at the time and, not aware of the liberation of women, left the university lest she "get ahead of her man."

Vienna during the First World War suffered from severe food shortages, inflation, and a revolution that overthrew the Hapsburg monarchy. A social democratic government was established that initiated programs of public housing, health, and welfare care that would set an example to the world. Being eighteen and an idealist, Elsa was caught up in the excitement of the utopian ferment and began taking evening classes at the Academy for Social Services. "I was quite idealistic and in a romantic way had world-saving goals . . . the whole period was one of idealism and I wanted to combine being a medical doctor with doing social work." She studied at the academy with August Aichorn, a well-known contemporary of Freud's, whose specialty was the study and treatment of delinquent children. His approach, she remembers, was quite the opposite from the accepted punitive methods of child-rearing of that time.

In 1930 Elsa married Fritz K., a relationship that lasted some eight years; it was dissolved just prior to her leaving Austria after the German invasion in 1938. For several years after they were married Fritz managed his uncle's business—selling gravestones —until he, too, became interested in medicine; the sacrifice her mother had been willing to make Elsa now made for her husband. During these years she supported the two of them as a social worker for the city of Vienna.

Then in March 1938 the bittersweet memories of Vienna were replaced by strutting Gestapo officers who changed the city overnight. "From the very beginning they would pull anybody off the streets who looked Jewish . . . and these people would just disappear. . . . I didn't look especially Jewish so I wasn't personally bothered. We used to make up stories in case we were arrested and asked what we were discussing. It was a very repressive and very frightening atmosphere. But the strange part was that there was still a lot of humor, black humor . . . you couldn't be upset all the time, it was impossible."

By November 1938 Elsa and her two sisters had managed to secure passports to come to America. But there was still another hurdle to be faced: in order to obtain an affidavit for residency in the United States, the applicant had to have a sponsor. "We knew that we had a distant cousin in the States, but he'd gone there thirty years ago and we were quite out of touch. Fortunately, my mother was a woman who kept addresses in her cupboard and so she wrote him a letter—to the last address she had which was a farm in Connecticut. By some miracle that letter followed him about until finally it caught up with him in the Bronx."

In looking back at her life, Elsa Leichter recognizes that she is a "second-chance person" and that America gave her that second chance. An experience she remembers most vividly is arriving in this country with her two sisters (she had separated from her husband, who remained in Europe) and traveling up to the Bronx to stay with the cousins they had never seen. "Nevertheless, they took us in, fed us and, because there were not enough beds, traded off with us, sleeping on the floor at night. Fortunately, that was only for a short period. There was an organization in New York which helped refugees find employment or educational opportunities; they thought I was good material and helped me get a scholarship in social work training at Western Reserve." She stayed there until 1941 when she came back to New York to work with the Jewish Family Services, where she worked until retiring in 1975.

In a sense, New York has always been a city of refugees. Among those Elsa met after the war was Otto Leichter, who had come there to reopen the German Press Agency at the United Nations. He was a Viennese widower in 1943 and for the next thirty years, "I was in some ways the little woman at home and at U.N. parties. My husband's professional work always took first place in our life." This second-chance marriage in no way needed the services of Elsa's profession. It was by any measure a happy, well-adjusted one. Her life with Otto changed Elsa's views, especially those relating to the country that had caused her family so much suffering. She says the change came because of her husband's work with the German Press Agency, "the most decent organization in the world, which was trying to give him something back, to compensate for the horrors that had been inflicted on his family."

As a psychotherapist, Elsa Leichter characterizes her work as being "integrationist." When studying at Western Reserve she was first trained in a largely psychoanalytic approach, working chiefly with individuals. Because psychology is an evolving discipline, Elsa has over the years maintained close contact with the changes and developments in the psychotherapeutic and social work field. Even now she attends workshops and seminars to remain current with the new approaches and ideas, and though interested in all areas of psychoanalytic techniques, she has attempted to integrate selectively those theories which she says "form a whole and which I constantly test out against the realities of practice and teaching. My main interest is working with couples and families that I view as systems—each member having an impact on the whole and each one affecting the workings of the others and each one perpetuating the patterns of the whole."

After Otto's death, Elsa's own pattern of life changed radically; she asked herself, "Who are you when 'you' have been 'we' for thirty years?"

In 1972, a year before her husband's death, the Director of the Psychoanalytic Institute in Hanover asked to meet Elsa in order to find out more about the latest developments in family therapy, a technique that was much more advanced here than in Germany. "I told him about my work in this country, and at the end of our discussion he asked me if I would be interested to come to Germany and conduct a seminar." The following year she received an invitation, but by then Otto had died and it wasn't until 1974, at the age of sixty-eight, that she went to Germany and began what was to be perhaps her most important work. Elsa was still sensitive to criticism from some that she was volunteering to help those who had treated her people so inhumanly. "I had to work something through for myself as well as with those I taught in Germany. . . . I realized that there was hardly one German family which hadn't experienced some loss and dislocation, and so there was the other side of the coin, where the trauma of those past years was still showing up in the grandchildren."

Mrs. Leichter chose to come to terms with the past and act as ombudsman between these families and the impact of their past. She admits that her decision was influenced by Otto Leichter's work with the German Press Agency which enabled him to meet a subsequent generation who in her words "were not responsible for their parents' sins." So each summer since 1974 she has returned to Germany to conduct seminars. As she was quoted in an interview given to Amy Gross, "What is important about the German work is that it is a rounding out of the most violently disruptive period of my life—leaving Austria. If you had asked me twenty years ago about some of the things I've seen in German families from working with them—their losses, their wanderings —I would have said it serves them right. Now I have fantastic friends out of the groups, in every city—exquisite friendships— and it is very meaningful for me to come back with what I have learned in America. I give them American thinking and practice as a gift and they receive it and give it back to me—it's very nourishing. There's been a real reconciliation. . . ."

Commenting on her work today in the States, she explains, "Families are my raw material." When conducting an interview, she and the family sit before an audience of twenty-five or more people in the psychotherapeutic field, all of them doctors, psychiatrists, or social workers. "I begin by saying to the family that we are now going on a trip and before we arrive at our destination it is hoped we will have discovered things that we did not know before." By watching and seeing things that Mrs. Leichter may miss, the audience supervises and supports her, learning all the time. The seminars last four days. Usually, a family comes about a problem with a child, but according to Elsa, "The child's disturbance is just a reflection of a problem between the parents. The child is merely the carrier, and some families are sophisticated enough to recognize this. Others do not understand it so I have to do a selling job. In families who, for example, have marital problems, even the so-called healthy child may find himself playing a certain role. Where the fight between the parents is not in the open, he often takes over and, by playing a certain role, maintains what we call a sick equilibrium. You must remember that all children are afraid that their parents' marriage will disappear and so they sacrifice themselves in order to keep them together."

According to Mrs. Leichter, one of the basic problems with today's marriages is that both partners are likely to enter into the relationship with their eyes tightly closed. The man often wants a mother who will be waiting for him at home with his slippers in one hand and a straight-up martini in the other. When all he gets are complaints about the children, and how the goddamned washing machine is on the fritz, his fantasized figure does what all mirages do when you get too close. As for the woman, she "often expects a husband who will take care of her and guess all her thoughts and wishes." Mrs. Leichter is not suggesting that we return to the twelfth century, when André le Chapelain, in *The Art of Courtly Love,* reminded us that "love can have no place between husband and wife"—only in extramarital affairs. Nor is she even arguing that ingredients other than love should be the epoxy that binds a marriage. What she is telling us is not to enter a marriage with the attitude: "I am not a whole person and that other person should hold me up lest I fall."

During Elsa's childhood, the Vienna of Sigmund Freud and August Aichorn was also the Vienna of Gustav Mahler, Johannes Brahms, Richard Strauss, and Arnold Schönberg, so it is not surprising that music is important. She had given up the piano at the age of fifteen when other causes seemed more important, but a half-century later, following Otto Leichter's death, she came back to the piano. She now plays several hours each day, loves Haydn, Schubert, Mozart, and particularly Bach, whose inventions she uses as her scales. She is giving the piano a second chance.

ELSA
LEICHTER

1905   *Born Elsa Schweiger in Vienna, Austria*

1923   *Began pre-med and social services studies at the University of Vienna*

1923–1938   *Worked with Dr. Aichorn in the Department of the City of Vienna Social Services*

1930   *Married Fritz K.*

1938   *Divorced Fritz K.*
     Emigrated to America

1939–1941   *Attended Western Reserve in Cleveland, Ohio*

1941–1975   *Member of Jewish Family Services; Family Therapy Consultant to Mt. Sinai, Beth Israel Hospital, Cancer Care; workshop leader and instructor in Multi-Family Group Therapy for American Group Psychotherapy Association, American Orthopsychiatric Society*

1943   *Married Otto Leichter*

1973   *Otto Leichter died*

1974–Present   *Conducts Seminars in Germany, Family Therapy at the German Psychoanalytic Institute of Hanover, Munich, Hamburg, and Bremen*

Vienna, where Leichter was born in 1905

Statue of Liberty, by which Leichter passed in 1938

Leichter and friends discuss new developments in family therapy

Bach, whose inventions she uses as her scales

Leichter today

Millicent McIntosh

"THE FAMILY COMES FIRST"

"If you must marry, plan to have babies in August so as not to interrupt your teaching careers." With a smile, Millicent Carey McIntosh recalls these words of her aunt, Carey Thomas, the President of Bryn Mawr College when she herself was an undergraduate there. President Thomas made a practice of speaking to the students in chapel three times a week. She would talk about her passion for reading, her devotion to scholarship, her fascination with travel, the intricacies of politics, and the rights of women.

Her niece has remained a disciple of the Gospel According to Thomas and is a deviant in only one detail. Although Mrs. McIntosh was to become one of our most distinguished college presidents, taking over the leadership of Barnard in 1952, her first allegiance has always been to her family. Perhaps this was because she herself came from a large family of six brothers and sisters. Perhaps it was because she loved children even more than she loved her work, or perhaps it was because she married a pediatrician who was enormously supportive of her career. Regardless of her reasons, by listening to her advice women today can learn a good deal about how to combine a career and a family without sacrificing one for the other.

Mrs. McIntosh recognized this early as an achievable goal. Her mother set the example by tending her six children and still finding time to sponsor such causes as women's suffrage, the peace movement, prison reform, and racial equality. "Her energy, her hard work on behalf of unpopular causes, made the deepest impression on me. I can't remember a time when I didn't expect to go to college to prepare myself to save the world," Mrs. McIntosh wrote in *Women and Success: The Anatomy of Achievement.*

It also helped that she came from stock in which the work ethic was deeply instilled. "I was one hundred percent Quaker. My mother's family, the Whitalls, had settled in Philadelphia in the eighteenth century, and both sides of my father's family, the Careys, settled in Baltimore during the same period, having been given a large land grant." Both her paternal and maternal grandfathers appear together in the portrait of the first Board of Trustees that hangs at Johns Hopkins University—one grandfather having been among the founders of the medical school, the other a founder of the university. The Bryn Mawr School in Baltimore, established to prepare young women to enter Bryn Mawr College, was founded by, among others, her aunt, M. Carey Thomas, who was dean of the college at the time. Both her mother and father were Quaker ministers, which meant that the young Miss Carey was not allowed to attend dancing class, go to the theater, or play cards on Sundays. It is thus not surprising that from early childhood she was bent on getting the education that would help her save the world. It is also not surprising that with this no-frills intellectual background, her views on education did not always jibe with the theories of progressive educators of that time.

Mrs. McIntosh has written, "Modern psychologists often claim that you cannot transfer learning skills; that sweating over Latin and math does not help you master other difficult tasks. I simply do not believe it; I am absolutely sure that the stiff requirements of my school and college made it possible to meet the arduous schedule I followed in my subsequent life. I feel grateful to the young Ph.D. who made us learn by heart the fifty principal parts of irregular Greek verbs and the highbrow English teacher who gave us endless lines of difficult poetry to memorize."

Because the conventional reaction to these tasks is likely to be rebellion rather than gratitude, it may have occurred to M. Carey Thomas that her niece had some unique intellectual properties which should be nurtured. By 1920, Miss Carey had graduated from college and was working for the Y.W.C.A., but she soon recognized, "You couldn't save the world through girls' clubs." So when Miss Thomas offered her a year abroad at Newham College, she abandoned charity for Cambridge University. Two years later she returned to Johns Hopkins to secure a doctorate, her thesis being a study of the English mystery plays known as the Wakefield Group of Towneley Cycle, a group of thirty-two plays written in 1460 and printed by a Lancashire family named Towneley. As the earliest English theater, the mystery plays were performances originally staged in the church and intended to convey the moral truths of Christian doctrine.

Millicent Carey, having now decided to save the world by teaching, returned to her alma mater as a member of the Bryn Mawr English Department, where she remained until 1930, when she became Headmistress of the Brearley School in Manhattan. It was during her second year there that she saw again a young Scotsman, Rustin McIntosh, a professor at Columbia College of Physicians and Surgeons who, while practicing pediatrics, had formed some definite ideas about motherhood. "Before we were engaged . . . when we first knew each other in Baltimore, he said that he had been convinced when practicing pediatrics that the worst mother was the twenty-four-hour mother, worse than the ordinary twenty-four-hour mother was the college graduate, and worst of all was a mother who had majored in psychology. . . .

129

Effective motherhood was not dependent on the amount of time the mother spends with her child, but on the quality of the time you give your children. He was really very far ahead of his time."

When Mrs. McIntosh talks about her husband of nearly fifty years, she has all the pride of a young bride who has read only the asset side of her mate's balance sheet. "He accepted women as equals (except women drivers) and he encouraged me to go on working after our children were born. He shared in the household tasks and made us able to have a truly liberated marriage. He's a very secure man. For instance, when the presidency of Bryn Mawr opened up in the late thirties, he said that if I wanted to apply for the job he would be glad to move to Philadelphia. I knew he had the best job in pediatrics in the country at the time, and the children were very young so I took my name right off the list." She is, of course, right to admire this quiet Scotsman who was secure enough in his own self-esteem to put his wife's career ahead of his own. Dr. McIntosh's offer demonstrates a form of generosity that has to be admired—as does his wife's refusal to accept it.

During her tenure at Brearley Mrs. McIntosh saw to it that the school not only maintained its reputation for rigorously pursuing academic excellence, but also insisted that students other than those whose families were listed in the *Social Register* be admitted into Brearley's hallowed halls. Snobbery was something she was least good at. Mrs. McIntosh is also a firm believer in the efficacy of athletics. Every afternoon between 2:30 and 4:30 her four hundred girls in their navy blue jumpers and white blouses would enter one of several gymnasiums. She liked her girls healthy, not only because they looked better, felt better, and tended not to have the vapors quite so often during Latin class, but also because they could have babies much later into life. She herself had her first pregnancy when she was thirty-four, making up for lost time by having twins. "I was married when I was thirty-three and my children were born between the time when I was thirty-four plus and the time I was forty-one. First there were the twins, then a girl and then two other boys in rapid succession. At one point we had four children under three years old. I was fortunate to have excellent health!"

"I have very strong convictions about marriage," Mrs. McIntosh said one winter morning as we talked together, looking over the snow-covered Massachusetts valley of Tyringham behind the cottage which she and her husband share in winter with their black Labrador, Pepper, and Cleopatra the cat. "If any conflict had arisen between my marriage and my career . . . if at any time I'd felt that my career was a threat to my family, I would have given it up overnight. And the message I kept repeating to the undergraduates at Barnard was that marriage is unique; if a choice has to be made and you choose to marry young and have children, then the important thing is to keep your mind alive . . . to keep your vocational interest alive by study or part-time work. Most of the students confused what I said with what I was able to do myself, not realizing that I had married late and had married a man who was particularly supportive of me. The message that seemed to come across to most of them was that they must have jobs, that they must have a career—which was not what I was trying to say to them at all."

Mrs. McIntosh has a practical reason for thinking that a woman who wants a family and a career should postpone marriage until she has established herself. "For if you marry young and have children, you have to face up to the fact that you can't work full-time." But she does not suggest that women should postpone marriage because a career is more important than a family —quite the opposite. She suggests postponing marriage because for her the family is far more important than a career, and there is simply no practical way to begin a career and at the same time to raise a family properly.

There is no doubt about Mrs. McIntosh's own priorities or

131

which of her accomplishments gives her the most satisfaction. She feels most satisfaction in the fact that her daughter is a history teacher and a cluster dean at Andover, while her daughter's husband is head of the Art Department and also teaches. She is also gratified that one son is an associate professor of English at Ann Arbor while his brother is Dean of Freshman and teaches linguistics at Brown, where his wife is a librarian. Another son is a doctor at the Harvard Medical School in charge of the study of contagious diseases while his wife is Deputy Director of Wellesley Women's Center, and her youngest son is a professor of biology at the University of Colorado while his wife teaches English history there.

She takes more satisfaction from all this than in the fact that she doubled Barnard's endowment and increased faculty salaries between 54 and 79 percent, broadened its curriculum, modernized its campus, created new courses, fought for women's rights, and has been awarded thirteen honorary degrees and has sat upon twenty-five boards.

The Drs. McIntosh retired in 1962 and, like everything else they did in their marriage, they did it together.

MILLICENT
MCINTOSH

(Right) Millicent, captain of varsity hockey team, Bryn Mawr, 1920

Breaking ground for Morningside Gardens, 1955

1898	Born Millicent Carey, Baltimore, Maryland
1920	A.B., Bryn Mawr College
1921–1922	Studied at Newham College, Cambridge University, England
1922–1923	English teacher, Rosemary Hall, Greenwich, Connecticut
1926	Ph.D., Johns Hopkins University, English
1926–1930	Member, English Department, Bryn Mawr College
1928–1929	Freshman Dean, Bryn Mawr College
1929–1930	Acting Dean, Bryn Mawr College
1930–1947	Headmistress, the Brearley School, New York
1932	Married Rustin McIntosh, M.D.
1933–1939	Twins James and Carey born, daughter Susan, and sons Kenneth and Richard born
1947	Dean of Barnard College, Columbia
1952	President, Barnard College; retained title and status of Dean in Columbia University.
1962	Retired as President, Barnard College, received title of President Emeritus, Barnard College, Dean Emeritus in Columbia University

Presidents of the seven sister colleges at Vassar, 1948

McIntosh with President Grayson Kirk at a commencement

The Doctors McIntosh

Madeline McWhinney

"A REFORMER
IN THE HALLS
OF MAMMON"

Even though Madeline McWhinney was only seven years old at the time of the stock market crash, she was well aware that our whole banking system had broken down. She was aware because her father who was part-owner of the International Trust Company in their hometown of Denver used to, on those long walks they took each Sunday afternoon over in Chessman Park, describe to her the difficulties that the country was going through. He did it in such a way that, rather than scaring her, it fascinated her. Madeline inherited his talent of making finance and economics, "that dismal science," as Thomas Carlyle called it, sound human, something that relates to people and not just to property.

As a member of the special honors group, Madeline graduated magna cum laude from Smith College in 1943, where she wrote a thesis on the devaluation of gold, which earned her a Phi Beta Kappa key. In 1943 she joined the Federal Reserve Bank, an organization established in 1913 to provide a mechanism to regulate the nation's supply of money and to control interest rates. At first she was rather overwhelmed by the job; in fact, after one

137

Linda Hackett

week, she told her mother she did not think she would survive. But McWhinney is made of stern stuff. When you hear that soft modulated voice start slowly and pick up speed, traversing backward and forward across the subject matter, explaining how she was hired "to develop a system of projecting what was happening in the money market as it related to day-to-day demands for currency and for gold, as well as to help the Treasury set the goals for the war bond drives," you begin to wonder if she is not a secret sharer in what E. F. Schumacher calls the "Buddhist" economic theory. Schumacher, a British economist who wrote *Small Is Beautiful,* defines it as a theory guided by the principle that work and leisure should not be antagonistic but complementary, both contributing to the development of the mind and body —to enable people to develop their faculties and not just turn out products.

While McWhinney may have been temporarily overwhelmed by her new responsibilities at the Federal Reserve Bank, she was willing to learn more. In her leisure time, she went to New York University night school because, as she says, "There was so much of the practical money market that I knew absolutely nothing about."

The area of the Fed that she was involved in had to do with statistics, the study of the movement of money, analytical work as it pertains to government securities, special studies requested by either Congress or the Fed's Board of Governors, and other such scholarly doings. That is not the way a great majority of the employees there spend each day, for the place is a big money factory where those on the assembly line while away the hours in sorting bonds, counting money, and arranging securities in neat little piles.

Madeline was perfectly happy to remain in her ivory tower and to write learned articles for the bank's prestigious *Monthly Review.* But her boss, Hobart Carr, thought to give his department a more "we're-all-in-this-together look" and asked her if she would run in the upcoming election to represent the employees in the Federal Reserve Pension Fund system, which embraced about 20,000 employees and had $161 million to watch over. "Just put your name in and forget about it," Carr told her. "There are dozens of others competing from the larger departments—they'll never elect you." What Hobart Carr had overlooked was that the New York manager of the Personnel Department, Frederick L. Smedley, had thrown his hat into the ring so that the entire remaining slate of candidates had, in deference to the respect they held for the gentleman and regard they had for their paychecks, withdrawn from contention. As Madeline says, "I didn't know enough to do that." Besides, there was this nice young man named Paul Volcker, who had worked for her in research and who was so enthusiastic about running her campaign that she did not want to disappoint him. Poor Mr. Smedley never know what hit him after Volcker, with his appetite for whimsy, organized a group of musicians from the people in research and paraded them through the employees' dining room during the lunch hour. In between meals, the two of them whistle-stopped in the other departments. "Well," Madeline says, *"The New York Times* got wind of these uncharacteristic banking practices, and sent reporters down, and we were in the papers all the time." She won hands down.

Paul Volcker, who would go on to become Chairman of the Federal Reserve Board, enjoyed himself but McWhinney did not, and that was the last time she ran for anything. She gives the appearance of being a rather shy woman, and politicking is obviously not her favorite form of exercise. From then on, any office she held would be one someone else had asked her to fill. And the offices that interested her most were those from which she could effect reforms.

By 1960, Madeline had been appointed as the first and only woman officer of the New York Federal Reserve Bank—one of the top banking positions in the country.

Among the reasons she resigned in 1973 to become the President of the First Women's Bank in Manhattan was that she believed women needed such an institution to guarantee them equal credit opportunities. However, even the most socially concerned of bankers has to realize when to demur; one of the problems the First Women's Bank had in their early days was their reluctance to say no, and some ridiculous loans were made. McWhinney admits that she was naïve about the role that the organizers of the bank had in mind for her. "What they wanted me for was to draw up a charter, get the deposits, and find a board of directors [which consisted of, among others, Betty Friedan, Jane Trahey, President of Trahey Advertising, Carol Greitzer, a New York City Councilwoman, and Alice Heyman, a member of the executive committee of the Ripon Society], to run the bank." In addition to making ill-advised loans, the bank spent too much money on expensive space and furnishings, but McWhinney could do nothing about that: the members of her board were not bankers but feminists and tended to overlook the fact that the bank was living beyond its means. Within six months they had a $400,000 operating deficit. But, whatever its shortcomings, the First Women's Bank did bring to a lot of people's attention the fact that women were being discriminated against in the halls of Mammon and some of these injustices were subsequently righted. The Equal Credit Opportunity Act was passed, women were given loans that would earlier have been denied them, and credit cards were issued to women who would not have been eligible before.

As Madeline McWhinney's reputation grew, her name became familiar outside banking circles, so when Governor Brendan Byrne of New Jersey needed to replace the Casino Control Commission, one of the five watchdogs he asked for was McWhinney. The New Jersey office is charged with licensing the casinos in Atlantic City, as well as everybody who works for them in any capacity, "from the president of the corporation down to the dishwashers."

"It's a very strange situation in New Jersey," Madeline says, folding her hands in her pearl-gray lap. "Originally, I had been told that the commission was very similar to the Federal Deposit Insurance Corporation or the Comptroller of the Currency, but they are independent while here the Governor and the New Jersey Legislature control everything we do. The whole operation is not to be believed. For instance, just consider the long set of criteria about financial stability, reliability, and ability to run a casino that the commission has to cope with. It even defines the minimum size of the hotel rooms connected with the casinos which must have a certain number of square feet, in addition to such-and-such amount of public space. We got a petition from one casino the other day that hasn't been able to attract enough people to their cabaret. They wanted to close it one night a week and show movies. But we can't let them because the law says they must have a cabaret and a bar with live entertainment. There's no flexibility. For instance, every company that sells to a casino must be licensed, the casinos themselves must be licensed, and in addition, we're supposed to be taking a leading role in ensuring that minorities receive an equal opportunity to work not only in the casinos but also in their construction. We're supposed to study the impact of casinos on Atlantic City, on housing, on transportation, on the environment. We are supposed to be doing something to turn Atlantic City back into a family tourist center in a place where the casinos are not the most important element—and we're supposed to be doing all this on casino money. It's wild—an uphill trip," she says, with a wry smile.

As a child, she used to ski in Aspen and Vail long before they had ski tows there. "You climbed uphill with skins on your skis, came down, and climbed up again. I was in pretty good condition because in the summers I used to mountain climb." She had climbed more than half the 14,000-foot mountains of Colorado by the time she was eighteen, so her legs were in good condition. Madeline McWhinney today still appears at ease with uphill trips.

MADELINE MCWHINNEY

McWhinney and Smedley run for Board of Trustees of the Reserve System's Pension Fund

1922	*Born Madeline McWhinney, Denver, Colorado*
1943	*A.B., Smith College*
1943–1973	*Economist, Federal Reserve Bank*
1947	*M.B.A., New York University Graduate School of Business Administration*
1955–1959	*Chief financial and trade statistician, Federal Reserve Bank*
1960	*Appointed first female officer, Federal Reserve Bank, New York*
1961	*Married John D. Dale*
1964	*Son Thomas Denny born*
1965–1973	*Assistant Vice-President, Federal Reserve Bank*
1974–1976	*President and Chief Executive Officer, First Women's Bank, New York City*
1976	*Member Casino Control Commission, New Jersey*
1977–Present	*Senior Consultant, Dale, Elliott & Company, New York*

McWhinney, President of First Woman's Bank, showing plan and scale model of bank, 1975

Promotional poster for First Woman's Bank

Meeting on casinos by gambling experts, 1982

Constance Baker Motley

"DUTY AND JUSTICE RIDING THE TIDE"

For Constance Baker Motley being first is nothing new. She was the first woman attorney to work with the National Association for the Advancement of Colored People, the first black woman member of the New York State Senate, the first and only woman to be President of the Borough of Manhattan, possibly the first black woman to argue a case before the United States Supreme Court, and the first black woman in the history of the Republic to be appointed to a Federal judgeship. Though this may be an awesome record of achievements, what, upon reflection, really impresses the observer is not her string of firsts but her compassion for the less privileged. In this she has for the past quarter of a century been the keeper of our conscience.

Motley is a big, majestic-looking woman who has retained some of the qualities of movement and gesture that three generations of her forebears acquired on the tiny Caribbean island of Nevis. That accounts for the serene, patient side of her nature, but there is the activist side of her character as well—honed on the streets of New Haven where she spent her childhood.

Linda Hackett

Her father, Willoughby Alva Baker, moved from Nevis to New Haven in 1906 and her mother a year later. They were married in 1907 and had twelve children, of whom nine survived. One went on to help make a reality of the American dream for many of her race.

Because Constance Baker had, from her earliest memories been concerned with the right of minorities she, even as a child, wanted to become a lawyer. Instinctively she seems to have laid the groundwork for a legal career by joining the high school debating society, the local political club, which led to becoming president of the youth council, and later, at the incredibly young age of fifteen, secretary of an adult organization known as the New Haven Community Council. The fact that she was black and a woman and came from a family unable to afford a college education—much less law school—made her chances to pursue such a career slim indeed. The story of how at eighteen she bootstrapped herself out of a life of mediocrity or worse would seem to be the stuff of "soaps."

Folding her hands, tilting her head ceiling-wise, and rocking back in her leather swivel chair, Judge Motley recounts the events that in 1940 led her to the position she occupies today. "After high school I got a job at the National Youth Administration which was sort of like the poverty program. The most I could have aspired to would have been to go to the local teachers' college and become an instructor, if it had not been for Clarence W. Blakeslee. Blakeslee, who owned the largest construction company in Connecticut, was among other things a philanthropist who had recently given the Dixwell Community Center to the black community for their recreation. You could have shot a moose in the place, it was so underutilized. Blakeslee called a meeting to determine what could be done to remedy the situation and when asked to speak I told the audience that the center was a failure because there were no blacks on the board and therefore the black community had no real input or interest in the project.

148

There were a lot of raised eyebrows and the blacks at the meeting thought that what I said was militant and embarrassing, but the next day Blakeslee told the director of the center to send me to him because he thought what I had said made sense. 'How come you are not in college?' he asked me. 'I have looked up your records and know that you graduated with honors from high school.' When I told him that I wanted to become a lawyer he said that he was skeptical about women going into that profession but in the end volunteered to send me not only to college but to law school as well." Five years later in 1946 she was graduated from Columbia Law School, having earned her B.A. from New York University two and a half years earlier. Constance Baker was twenty-four and Mr. Blakeslee eighty-four when he attended her graduation.

In her senior year at Columbia, Motley got a job as a clerk with the Legal Defense Fund, whose parent association is the National Association for the Advancement of Colored People. As she confides, "I was very lucky to be in on the ground floor of what was to develop into the biggest legal office in the country." In 1945 when she began clerking there the firm consisted of three principals: Thurgood Marshall, who went on to become a Justice of the United States Supreme Court, Edward Dudley, who is today a New York State Supreme Court Judge, and Robert Carter, who, like Motley, is also a Federal Judge. In 1946, the Legal Defense Fund was concentrating on helping blacks obtain employment in defense industries and fighting segregation in the armed forces. During the war blacks had joined the N.A.A.C.P. in record numbers for they felt resentment not only against segregation in the armed forces but also the court-martial proceedings which they believed often imposed stiffer sentences on blacks.

One must speculate that it was the patient side of her nature that held Motley in check when, as a young law clerk with the Legal Defense Fund, she reviewed the stacks of courts-martial that had been meted out to blacks after the Second World War, something she could hardly have perceived as fair. But it was the activist that would help redress these and other grievances. Thurgood Marshall believed that the unhealthy race relations that had led to this unequal rendering of justice were traceable to segregation in education, and unless integrated schools became a reality, racial inequalities would continue. "When I finished law school in 1946 the N.A.A.C.P. decided that because the poor treatment blacks suffered during the war had received a good deal of publicity, they would pick up on the progress that had been made and strive to get segregation in the society wiped out by challenging the concept of segregation in schools," Motley stated.

Segregation became the law of the land back in 1896 when the Supreme Court ruled that the state of Louisiana had the power to provide separate but equal railroad accommodations for blacks traveling within the state. As a result, the doctrine of separate but equal was dignified and later grafted onto the school system of the South. But the graft was rejected by the country a half-century later in a series of events that should dispel any doubt in the reality of poetic justice.

For example, the state of Missouri in 1938 had but one state-supported law school and when Lloyd Gaines, a black man, asked admission he was rejected and offered an out-of-state scholarship —a sleight-of-hand method of complying with separate but equal Federal requirements. The case went to the Supreme Court, which ruled that a state could not meet its obligations by simply exporting blacks to out-of-state schools even though they would foot the bill for the difference in cost. The state of Missouri now found itself in the ironic position of either accepting Gaines at its university or having to build a one-man law school for him. So much for poetic justice.

But they did neither. So much for law and order.

The question was not raised again until a young black woman by the name of Ada Lois Sipuel petitioned to enter the University of Oklahoma in 1946 and the court ruled that the states had an obligation to provide not only equal protection within their borders but equal education at the same time. Oklahoma then finally admitted Miss Sipuel to the state's only law school. The neighboring state of Texas was facing a similar problem raised by a black man named Sweat and his was the first case that Motley worked on. Texas had followed Oklahoma's example but with a twist: it set up a personalized law school in the basement of a building in Austin, Texas, sent over some law books, and assigned four professors from the University of Texas law faculty to instruct young Sweat. It was crazy, and the Supreme Court told Texas as much by saying that one of the ingredients for a legal education is the opportunity to confer with other prospective members of the bar and so ordered his admission to the university. That was the first time the Court had directed a previously all-white institution to accept a black student. Back in Oklahoma they found a better solution than building an entire university for just one student. Why not just quarantine him or her in a room adjoining the regular classroom and assign him or her a private table in the library and dining room? That's what they did to G. W. McLaurin, who was going after his master's in education. But the Supreme Court would not buy that ruling either, declaring it was illegal to segregate someone within an institution. Motley worked on both these cases.

In 1954, Motley's first case to end up in the Supreme Court was *Brown vs. Topeka, Kansas, Board of Education*, which struck down racial intergration in public education. Because it involved elementary schools and the Court had ruled that segregation in public educational institutions was unconstitutional, the decision foreshadowed the end of segregation in all other public places and set the stage for future civil rights desegregation cases. Motley would argue ten cases before the Supreme Court, winning nine. But not all of her battles were fought in the relative safety of the Northeast corridor, for Mrs. Motley had to make forays into the Deep South where she would try cases ranging from busing in Jackson, Mississippi, to segregated restaurants in Memphis, to whites-only lunch counters in Birmingham, to Martin Luther King Jr.'s right to conduct a march in Albany, Georgia.

As events would prove, it was dangerous down there in the '6os. She remembers driving one dawn between Jackson and Meridian with Medgar Evers and her secretary Roberta Thomas when they came upon a stretch of lonely road bracketed by cypress and live oaks covered with Spanish moss and half hidden by the early morning mist rising out of the swamp. Medgar said to her, "Don't look back. We're being followed, and we're the only car on the road." The car followed them for an hour and it was only when they arrived in Meridian that they discovered the driver was a state trooper in an unmarked car. "We were frightened to death, but to this day it is unclear why he followed us." She remembers other things that frightened her, such as sitting in a living room across the street from Evers's house and looking at the bush in front of his door. That bush terrified her. As she later said, "Those streets were unpaved in the black community of Jackson and Medgar's house was in the fork of the road which had this bush growing on it with his house right behind. I remember we discussed how someone could hide behind that bush at night and shoot him and that's exactly what happened. . . . And we knew that it would happen.

"I remember the first case against the University of Alabama in 1955. We stayed in Arthur Shore's house [Arthur Shore was the N.A.A.C.P. lawyer in Birmingham] and it was guarded by guys with machine guns and rifles because it had been bombed so many times. At the time I worked with James Meredith to get him into the University of Mississippi, he used to carry a cane to protect himself, so in fear was he for his life. When he finally did get into the University of Mississippi, the government assigned a Federal marshal to sleep in his room for the entire year he was there. Yes, we were in fear much of the time. . . ."

And this is where her sense of fairness is again revealed for even though there were life or death issues involved she admits to having admiration for some of those who disagreed with her position. She recalls in particular Judge Sidney Meis who presided over the Meredith case. "Meis was a very urbane and civilized man who was not filled with hate or anger against the blacks. . . . He was fearful for us because he knew what was coming and was hoping that he would never have to decide it. . . . In the end he had to, though. He ruled against ending segregation in Mississippi's schools."

As her assistant for the last twenty years, Roberta Thomas, says, "We admired some of the opposing lawyers—they were good, but we just wished that they had been on our side."

"What we had on our side," suggested Judge Motley one morning, "was duty and justice riding the tide."

But Motley recognizes that duty and justice without compassion are like a tripod with two legs. There is a story that demonstrates how she reconciled the three elements. A young heroin addict came before her one day for selling heroin and it was her duty to commit him to the Federal penitentiary for a period of years and in this justice was served. At the time of the sentencing she noted that the lad's arms were scarred from the numerous times he had injected heroin. She made a mental note of this and later wrote letters to the parole board asking if some form of plastic surgery could not be performed on his arms for, as she explained, "Once a free man, no one would ever hire him with these telltale signs of addiction." It is sad to report that nothing was done.

Judge Motley no longer believes that our most pressing problem is segregation. This, through the Federal courts, has been solved, but in resolving that legal issue other problems have been created. As she said in a speech to the Women's Law Caucus at the University of Montana's Law School, "The greatest handicap today is no longer race, but poverty. . . ." One of the "realities of American life today is that most of our urban centers are growing both blacker and poorer. This has resulted not only from middle-class whites fleeing desegregated schools in the South and predominately black schools in the North, but from the fact that our central city housing is old and dilapidated and new housing in the suburbs has generally been beyond the financial reach of most blacks and poor whites." Because of "the legal success of the Civil Rights movement, it has brought new petitioners to the Federal courts who in turn seek a new definition of justice. Like civil rights, welfare rights is now a new discipline in the law . . . and in this connection a new group of legal craftsmen are looking for justice for the poor."

Seated behind her great desk, big as a Chippendale writing table, in chambers whose walls house a thousand or more law manuals, Motley cautions the visitor that "social change is everywhere." And for her those shelves of law manuals are the front line from which she battles for this change. The Judge believes that the Federal courts have become the "center for social-conflict resolution in American society . . . and that the law has been the single most effective catalyst for change in twentieth-century America."

She rises, Roberta Thomas helps her on with her robes, she waves goodbye, and proceeds briskly down the corridor and into a court where she will preside. Watching this regal woman recede, the visitor becomes aware that he has been in the company of a being who personifies the majesty of the law.

CONSTANCE
BAKER MOTLEY

Motley, 1967

1921	*Born Constance Baker, New Haven, Connecticut*
1943	*B.A., New York University*
1946	*LL.B., Columbia University*
1946	*Married Joel Wilson Motley*
19?	*Son Joel born*
1945–1965	*Member of legal staff of N.A.A.C.P. Legal Defense and Educational Fund*
1948	*Admitted to the New York Bar*
1954	*Argued* Brown vs. Board of Education *before Supreme Court*
1958–1964	*Member of the New York State Advisory Council on Employment and Unemployment Insurance*
1964–1965	*Member of New York State Senate*
1965–1966	*President of Manhattan Borough*
	LH.D., Smith College; LL.D., Western College for Women and Morehouse College
	U.S. District Judge, Southern District of New York
1966–1976	*LL.D., Howard University; West Virginia State College; Morgan State College; Iowa Wesleyan University; Fordham University; Brown University; Albertus Magnus College*

Martin Luther King, whose right to conduct a march in Albany, Georgia, Motley defended

Foley Square North, where Motley presides

Judge Motley today

Betty Parsons

"HER GALLERY IS A PLACE WHERE ART GOES ON"

> When the music flows
> And no voice is heard
> Like a plant that grows
> Like a soundless bird
>> Betty Parsons

W. Somerset Maugham once made the point that writers may respect all forms of literature, but it is the poets of whom they remain in awe. The poet has to have a touch of the mystic and see things a little differently from the rest of us . . . perhaps clearer than the rest of us, or from another angle than the rest of us . . . or maybe just sooner than the rest of us. A poet can divine a thing instinctively which the rest of us must be taught. This may be one reason Betty Parsons understood a movement in American art that was later labeled Abstract Expressionism, or the New York School, long before any of her contemporaries. Of course it helped that she is an artist herself, but the main reason was that she is also a poet.

"I remember," Betty Parsons says, "spending a weekend at Lady Redding's place in Sussex. I was painting inside the greenhouse when Lady Redding came in and looked and said she didn't see what on earth I saw to make me paint like that. I said, 'That flower excites the hell out of me, and I'm trying to paint that excitement.' She saw right away what I meant."

Lady Redding may have been a better student than the American public, or most of the art critics, back in 1946, when Mrs. Parsons opened her gallery at 15 East 57th Street in Manhattan and tried to explain to them why the work of Jackson Pollock and Clyfford Still and Barnett Newman and Mark Rothko and Hans Hofmann and Ad Reinhardt was important. Almost nobody could appreciate their worth, and it took about twenty years for the poet's message to penetrate. "Rothko, Pollock, Still, all came out of the great big enormous West and what they were painting was the expanding world. It is interesting to compare their work with, say, Picasso, who used everything and recreated it in his own image, so to speak. . . . He was supremely inventive, but he could no more paint like the Americans than he could fly. It is because he lived in Europe, which to me is like a walled city, whereas those Americans came from our enormous West and lived in an expanding world and painted that world . . . they were influenced by our vastness."

I asked Parsons what had influenced her the most and, without hesitation, she replied, Chartres Cathedral. "I was terribly depressed then, and I didn't think much of man. I thought he was awfully mean, but when I saw Chartres Cathedral, I said man must have something marvelous about him to have created this, and that had an enormous influence on me." She was a young woman when this happened, on her honeymoon with her husband, Schuyler Livingston Parsons, both of them straight out of the F. Scott Fitzgerald blue-blazer background of Newport, Eastern prep schools and debutante parties, polo playing, yacht racing, flappers, Lindy hopping, and hard drinking. Neither Betty's friends nor her parents understood or cared much for art, and both at the Chapin School in New York and later at Miss Randall McKeever's finishing school, art was something quite outside of the curriculum.

Her mother was from New Orleans, and is said to have been blessed with marvelous taste and cursed with inordinate extravagance. Her father, Frederick Rhodes Pierson, who was brought up on the family property in Ramapo, New York, not only lacked taste, but also talent for business. Between her mother's extravagance and her father's poor business judgment, such as trying to corner the coconut market (a commodity that most of us can live without), the family had forfeited the bulk of their fortune by the time Betty was married in 1919.

The year before, Betty had been given permission by her parents, who did not believe in college for girls, to study with Gutzon Borglum, the man who harassed Mount Rushmore with the busts of our Presidents, and what he did to our environment he also did to Betty. "He was so conservative that he would permit me to draw bones only from pictures in a book. . . . I wasn't allowed even to approach the real thing. I remember when I was thirteen my nurse took me to the Armory Show. I knew then and there that I wanted to be an artist. I recognized that these men and women were trying to say something beyond just demonstrating an ability to copy a peach."

After the honeymoon, when she and Schuyler returned to New York, Mrs. Parsons began to study sculpture with Mary Tonetti, a form of expression to which she still feels closest. She also attended the Parsons School of Design (no connection to her husband's family), and was offered a job as a clothes designer, but rejected it when her in-laws objected. She claims, "In retrospect, it is fortunate that they did or I may well have devoted my life to that field." Her marriage to Schuyler lasted two years. Their divorce in 1923 led to an acrimonious discussion of the sanctity of marriage between Betty and her grandfather, who would commemorate the first divorce in the family by disinheriting her. Later her mother raised the count to two by divorcing her father, and like Betty, moved to Paris. Parsons lived there for ten years and her mother until the Second World War forced her to return reluctantly to America. The decision to move there was not because they wanted to be together. Far from it. They saw each other only at Christmas and Thanksgiving. "My mother simply didn't understand my life and hers to me was an anathema. I was, at the time, studying with Antoine Bourdelle at the Grande Chaumière . . . Giacometti was in the same class . . . we were both so shy that it was months before we spoke, and then only after Bourdelle had said that we were the only ones who were trying to say something about the model. That gave me the courage to go on."

It was the perfect time for a young artist to study in Paris. Betty lived at 29 rue Boulard with a studio on the rue Perceval. Her small alimony from Schuyler Parsons continued for the next few years until, like her father, he, too, became a victim of the crash in 1929. By then she had met Isamu Noguchi, Tristan Tzara, Gertrude Stein, Alice B. Toklas, Harry Crosby, Man Ray, Gerald and Sara Murphy, among others and, alimony or not, she was determined to remain in Paris.

While the loss of an alimony check was inconvenient, it was probably not as devastating to Betty as it would have been for most young American women living alone in the City of Lights. She spoke the language perfectly and moved in a circle of artists where the thought of money only surfaced when the rent was due or the wine ran low. She was completely sure of herself and her antecedents; so being poor, while not all that agreeable, created no psychic problems for her. "She seemed," as Jeanne Reynal, a friend of Betty's who has shown at the Parsons Gallery, once said, "like one of those great English aristocrats who take for granted who they are." Another friend called her "the last of the elegant bohemians."

Two of Parsons's friends of this period were Amedeo Modigliani, who was never to earn recognition during his lifetime, and Alexander Calder, who was to become widely known a few years hence. But at that time almost no one outside of their immediate circle recognized Calder's talent. "Sandy and I used to go dancing at least once a week. . . . I remember one evening when rather than dancing he took a group of us back to his studio. We all sat on boxes while he manipulated the acrobats, clowns, tightrope walkers, and the rest that were part of his just completed circus. I still laugh when I go to the Whitney and see the now famous circus on the first floor there in that Plexiglass box. I laugh not only because the genius of the piece is that he created it to give us cheer, and it still does, but also I remember what fun we had when we first played with it a half-century ago."

Parsons had her first show at the Grand Chaumière and Janet Flanner reviewed it for *The New Yorker*. Some things were sold and she earned her first money as an artist. She could have earned more of it, easier and faster, if she had become a model for Schiaparelli, which she was asked to do. Or if she had driven a Citroen—with a woman friend of her choosing—all the way from the Polish border across Russia to Vladivostok, as the manufacturers had urged her to do. Betty, who during this period had the distinction of being constantly mistaken for Greta Garbo, was obviously capable of selling anything from high fashion to touring cars. Neither interested her.

What did interest her was her work with Ossip Zadkine, the sculptor, whom she studied with after Bourdelle, primarily "to learn how to use various kinds of sculpture material that no one else employed." (In the 1970s the material Betty would choose to make her own statement would be a material that no one else had used, or at least used in the same way. Her special material is driftwood, collected on the beach in Southold, Long Island, which she paints with acrylic colors and fits together into what can perhaps be best described as sculptured paintings. Like Calder's work, it is joyous.)

During the summers she and a group of friends, including the English artists Adge Baker and Arthur Lindsay, with whom she studied the technique of watercolor, would go to Normandy where Betty painted scenes of fishing villages and harbors filled with tiny boats flying the tricolor. The reds and blues of the French flag are still central to her palette.

Betty Parsons would have probably gone on living in France if circumstances had permitted, and in fact, she did manage to remain in Paris until 1933, four years after receiving her last alimony payment. From time to time, she would rent her apartment to friends and travel across the Channel to England for the summer. Augustus John was an old friend, and she recalls arriving at his house in the country for the weekend to find that all the windows had been flung open and in each appeared the face of one of the many children he had sired during his notorious career.

Returning to Paris from one of these trips, she discovered that a telephone had been installed at 29 rue Boulard by her mother. Now a telephone has never been the instrument of communication that Mrs. Parsons respects the most, and as a matter of fact she has never allowed one to be installed in her house on the island of St. Martin. Her view is that if one cannot converse face to face, then the next best means of communication is to send a handwritten message. "I would rather send smoke signals than talk on the telephone," she once confided. What her mother had gained in easier communication she had lost in access for Betty did not talk to her for three months after the incident.

When in 1933 she did return to this country, it was not to New York but, on the advice of friends, to California. She drove alone in a Model-T Ford across the continent. It might not have been as exciting as the transcontinental trip that Citroen had proposed she take across Russia, but then Santa Barbara offered somewhat more opportunity for a young artist than did Vladivostok. But not a whole hell of a lot, because in order to live, she had to take a job in a liquor shop. Alexander Archipenko, the Russian sculptor, had also settled in California and Betty studied with him in Los Angeles during this period. Here, her old friend Robert Benchley introduced her to the film colony. But California was not her "cup of tea" and so in 1938 she sold her wedding ring for $1,000 and returned to New York.

"I have always called it my destiny. . . . I have certainly never thought of it as moving into the right place at the right moment." Her destiny is a poet's sense, Robert Browning's sense, if you will, of being able to "seize the moment." The group of artists who, for lack of a better name, were to be labeled Abstract Expressionists, was beginning to coalesce there. For the previous twenty-five years, she had been showing her own work at the Midtown Galleries, but the sales were too small to support even her very modest existence, so when the gallery director Alan Gruskin suggested that she might organize exhibitions and sell for the Midtown on a commission basis, she accepted.

A year later, Mrs. Cornelius J. Sullivan, one of the founders of the Museum of Modern Art, asked Betty to join her 460 Park Avenue gallery, which exhibited many of the paintings of the Impressionists and Post-Impressionists such as Monet, Matisse, and Betty's old friend Modigliani, now dead. She remained there a year, but sometime in the spring of 1940 the Phipps family who owned the Wakefield Book Shop on East 55th Street, offered her some empty space in the basement in which to establish a gallery. That was a turning point in Betty's life.

For the first time she was mistress of her own ship, so to speak, and could sail to any port of her choosing. She chose to sail it into the future by showing the works of young unrecognized artists who had in her view creative potential. During the next four years she introduced Walter Murch, Alfonso Ossorio, Joseph Cornell,

Saul Steinberg, Hedda Sterne, Constantino Nivola, and Adolph Gottlieb. Gottlieb had exhibited his Surrealist work previously, but it was at the Wakefield that his first abstract pictures appeared. When the Wakefield moved uptown in 1944 Betty accepted an offer from Mortimer Brandt to become director of a new section of his Old Masters Gallery, which was to concern itself with the work of contemporary artists. Ad Reinhardt, Mark Rothko, Hans Hofmann, and Theodoros Stamos (who had previously been shown at the Wakefield) were among them.

Almost nothing was sold and, within two years, Brandt decided to retrench and return to Old Masters, leaving Betty with the space at 15 East 57th Street to do with what she wanted. In the fall of 1946, the Betty Parsons Gallery was opened on $5,000 of which $1,000 was hers, the remaining being loans from four friends.

Virtually the only other gallery in Manhattan interested in showing the works of contemporary artists at this time was Peggy Guggenheim's Art of this Century, which had opened in 1942 and had exhibited, among other Americans, the work of Jackson Pollock. In 1947, Miss Guggenheim decided to close her gallery and move to Venice. Jackson Pollock, Mark Rothko, Barnett Newman, and Clyfford Still, who wanted to remain together as a group, asked Betty to represent them. "I remember that I had taken a cottage in Provincetown that summer. It was near Curt Valentin's, the most respected art dealer in New York at the time. One day he asked me what I thought of this new group of artists, and when I said that I thought that their work was fascinating, he responded, 'I must be going blind.' "

Mrs. Parsons has always returned to the past for an exhibition to inaugurate a new gallery introducing contemporary art. At the Wakefield she showed pre-Columbian stone sculpture; at the East 57th Street gallery, she mounted an exhibition of Northwest Coast Indian art; and when she moved to her last gallery on West 57th Street, her first show was a 2,000-year-old sculpture that had recently been discovered in Amlash, Iran. There was a deliberate message in these exhibitions, explained by Barnett Newman, the spokesman and the intellectual force behind the Abstract Expressionist movement.

"It is becoming more and more apparent that to understand modern art, one must have an appreciation of the primitive arts, for just as modern art stands as an island of revolt in the stream of Western European esthetics, the many primitive art traditions stand apart as authentic esthetic accomplishments that flourished without benefit of European history. . . . There is an answer in these works to all those who assume that modern abstract art is the esoteric exercise of a snobbish elite, for among these simple peoples, abstract art was the normal, well-understood, dominant tradition. Shall we say that modern man has lost the ability to think on so high a level? Does not this work rather illuminate the work of those of our modern American abstract artists who, working with the pure plastic language we call abstract, are infusing it with intellectual and emotional content, and who, without any limitation of primitive symbols, are creating a living myth for us in our own time?"

Newman was a most articulate, gregarious man, always dressed like a banker, complete with vest, monocle, watch fob and chain stretched across his generous stomach. When he was not formulating the postulates on which much of the abstract movement's esthetic would rest, he would be off at Stillman's Gym watching young Puerto Ricans train for Saturday night boxing matches or giving tours of City Hall to point out some of the most interesting features about the murals. He loved City Hall to such a degree that he ran for mayor against La Guardia in 1933.

In the beginning, Newman, Rothko, Pollock, Still, and Reinhardt were all close friends. They would meet on Saturday nights at the Parsons Gallery and help in the hanging of one another's shows, after which they would all go down to the Village for dinner. Parsons recalls that before one show Rothko wanted to hang more pictures than the wall space could accommodate so he and the sculptor Tony Smith, along with some other friends, spent the night building a free-standing wall on which to hang them. It was not unlike Rothko to want to get the most for his money or, to be more precise, the most for Betty Parsons's money, for at that time he had not yet begun to sell. That would begin to happen about two years after he had left her gallery. Tony Smith, who a few years later became famous for his massive black geometric sculpture, was also an architect, and built the house on Long Island Betty Parsons loves so dearly. She had inherited $40,000 from an uncle, which she handed to Smith before leaving for Europe in July 1959, and said she'd be returning in September and hoped that he could have the house at least partially completed by then. No plans . . . no specs . . . no limitations . . . no restrictions . . . or instructions, just a poet's faith that a fellow artist would know the type of studio that she needed. She later wrote this about his sculpture:

> The sky looked down
> and all around
> the earth was under
> something grand
> it was not rock
> it was not sand
> it was the scale
> upon the land
> that reached the summit
> of the light
> and tossed the day
> upon the night.

The Parsons Gallery had more the flavor of a cooperative than a commercial venture and artists felt at ease there, so much so that Pollock, Rothko, Newman, and Still came to Mrs. Parsons proposing that she concentrate on them to the exclusion of other artists; together they would make her "the most famous dealer in the world." While she knew that fame would be the probable result of such a collaboration, she also sensed that it would not work and so rejected the idea on the grounds that she did not "like a small garden." Her instinct was correct, for within a very short time the four men were not speaking to each other; Newman was suing Reinhardt for slander, Pollock was going his own lone way in Springs at the end of Long Island, and Still refused to exhibit anywhere until almost twenty years later in 1969. The only one of the group to remain with Parsons throughout his life was Ad Reinhardt. On the day of the opening of an exhibition, the following reference was made to Reinhardt's work in Betty's diary:

> The rooms opened to another shore
> between the waves of night
> where darkness ever folds itself
> within the waves of light.

If her artists were unified during those first few years in defense of each other's work, the critics were equally united in rejecting it. Stuart Preston of *The New York Times* said to her after Newman's first show, "Betty, any more shows like that and they will throw you off the street." Later, when he returned to the gallery as a Clyfford Still exhibition was in progress, "He got off the elevator," as Betty describes it, "took one look and began to return to the elevator. . . . I actually dragged him back into the gallery and asked him to spend five minutes alone with the work . . . please. He remained and upon leaving grudgingly admitted that maybe there was something to the work after all. John Canaday of the *Times* was often very harsh on my artists. . . . I am fond of John, in fact spent my seventy-fifth birthday dancing with him all night, but he didn't much like what was going on in the contemporary art world." But she also had some supporters. Alfred Barr, Director of the Museum of Modern Art, and Dorothy Miller, the chief curator, "were really the ones who supported me all along." Also, some of the more receptive collectors, such as Ben Heller, Mrs. Burton Tremaine, Edward Root, and Duncan Phillips were beginning to buy the work of some of her artists.

In 1956, ten years after the opening of the Parsons Gallery, Barnett Newman made a selection of the twenty-five artists who had exhibited during that period and Tony Smith hung the work. By then, Abstract Expressionism was well established as an important school and the show was reviewed by the critics with almost universal acclaim. As Clement Greenberg noted in the announcement for the show, many of the artists who had started with her had moved on to other galleries, "but a large measure of the prestige . . . that is now theirs rebounds upon her. . . ." Pollock and Rothko had gone across the hall to the Sidney Janis Gallery; Still contemplated going to Janis but then thought better of it and went nowhere; Newman was bitterly hurt by the reviews of his 1951 show at Parsons, and that, along with lack of support from his fellow artists, caused him to stop showing his work for the next eight years. But other artists had, and would for years, continue to take their place: Bradley Walker Tomlin, Alexander Liberman, Anne Ryan, Robert Rauschenberg, Lee Krasner, Calvert Coggeshall, Richard Tuttle, William Congdon, Kenzo Okada, Lee Hall, Richard Lindner, Cleve Gray, and Ellsworth Kelly, to mention a few. In fact, by 1958, the popularity of the gallery among artists was such that Betty began a second gallery next door known as Section Eleven. It remained open for the next four years until it became apparent that the physical gallery and the person of Parsons were so intertwined and part of a whole that even the smallest physical separation between them was unworkable. However, during the years it remained open, it did give gallery space to unrecognized talent which is not the way most dealers like to ration out their walls. Among others, Agnes

Martin, Ruth Volmer, Sven Lukin, and Aline Porter were exhibited there.

Unlike most galleries, Parsons has never offered its artists a contract. This is partly due to the fact that Betty has not had the financial resources to underwrite contracts, but mainly because she does not want to taint the gallery's atmosphere with lawyers and accountants. Another rule adhered to throughout the years is never allowing her own work to be shown in the gallery. "I have never felt my own work should be exhibited at Parsons because there must be a clear line between what I create and what I sell. As an artist I want someone else to decide that they wish to or do not wish to show my work. While I will be the judge of my work I refuse to be the jury." Many artists shown by Mrs. Parsons have moved on to other galleries that would offer them a contract and all the security that entails, but of them all, there were only two with whom she had a disagreement: Clyfford Still and Ellsworth Kelly. In both cases it had to do with their moving to the Sidney Janis Gallery. In Still's case, Betty was hurt by the fact that she had heard rumors from others that he was going to follow Pollock and Rothko to Janis. When she wrote him a letter saying, "You didn't have the courage to tell me that you had signed up with Sidney Janis," she received an angry reply, which led to a break in their relationship for many years. In 1963 when Ellsworth Kelly decided to move on, Betty told him he was free "to go any place he liked" but that she would never talk to him again if he chose Sidney Janis. Ellsworth Kelly did go on to Janis and true to her word, they did not speak for years, but Betty Parsons is inconstant in enmity, and in time, they became fast friends once more.

Parsons, however, is totally constant about the way her galleries should look; she believes that the exhibition space must be left unadorned. No felt-draped walls, pile carpets, chrome fixtures; her galleries are Yankee plain enough to make her Protestant forebears almost forgive her for her taste in art. "The gallery is not what we are exhibiting here . . . it is the artist's work that is important." And when she moved to West 57th Street in 1963 she maintained the spartan look of her previous galleries.

Clement Greenberg has commented that her gallery "is a place where art goes on and is not just shown and sold." The same thing can be said about her life. Perhaps that is why she has been able to make such a unique contribution to the art of the present. If she had established her gallery with a bottom-line priority rather than a place "where art goes on" there could have been no justification for showing artists whose talent was unrecognized. That made no business sense. But like Kingman Brewster, the late President of Yale, Betty believes in "looking below the bottom line" and in this her convictions have made sense. David Herbert, an assistant she hired just after he had graduated from college, remembers "I came to New York armed with all sorts of letters and Betty hired me after twelve others had said no. She did not want to read any of the letters, preferring just to talk to me and trust her own instinct." It was, of course, this instinct for recognizing talent before others that would make her famous among artists and collectors. The gallery has been able to play a key role in the world of contemporary art not because Betty chose artists whose work might immediately sell, but because she gave young talent a chance. In 1973, on an African safari, Mrs. Parsons sat day after day sketching the animals while the four-wheel-drive vehicle bounced over the Serenghetti or rested in front of a pride of lions. One day while visiting a camp of the Masai she painted in her diary some small watercolor of the tribe in their long magenta robes. In work done after that trip it can be seen how her palette and line were influenced by the colors and patterns she had observed. Earlier, in 1947, she went to a rodeo in California and painted her first abstract picture in order to capture all the noise, action, and colors of the day. Some of her most successful works are her driftwood pieces. They combine her original love of sculpture with her strong sense of color applied to a humble material that conveys an admiration for the primitive. In 1947 for a show at her gallery entitled "The Ideographic Picture," Barnett Newman wrote in the foreword of the catalog: "There is a new force in American painting that is the modern counterpart of the Primitive Art impulse." He could have been addressing his words to these wooden pieces for they are indeed "the modern counterpart of the primitive art impulse"—an art where, to quote Betty Parson's own lines:

> We arrange nothing
> things happen
> the picture with the blue window
> looking at eternity
> remains as a spirit

BETTY PARSONS

1900   Born Betty Pierson, New York City
1913   Attended the Armory Show
1918   Studied drawing with Gutzon Borglum
1919   Married Schuyler Livingston Parsons
1920   Studied sculpture with Mary Tonetti

Betty at five

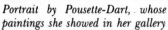

Portrait by Pousette-Dart, whose paintings she showed in her gallery

Betty, by Saul Steinberg, 1958

            Attended Parsons School of Design
1922   Divorced Schuyler Parsons
1923   Moved to Paris
1932   Her work shown at Grand Chaumière Gallery
1933   Returned to the States and drove to Santa Barbara, California
1933–1935   Studied sculpture with Alexander Archipenko
1938   Returned to New York
1938–1939   Director of Cornelius Sullivan Gallery

Parsons loved animals

Studio in Southold, Long Island, built by the sculptor Tony Smith

1940–1943 Director of Wakefield Gallery
1943–1946 Director of Contemporary Section of Old Masters Gallery
1946 Director of Betty Parsons Gallery
1947–1982 One-woman shows of her work at Midtown Galleries; Miami Museum; New Art Gallery, Atlanta; Bennington; Gallery 7, Boston; Grand Central Modern, New York City; White Chapel Gallery, London; Studio Gallery, Washington, D.C.; Sachs Gallery, New York City; Drew University; Benson Gallery, Bridgehampton, Long Island, New York; David Hendriks Gallery, Dublin, Ireland; Kornblee Gallery, New York City
1977 U.S.I.A. Traveling Exhibition, Louise Himelfarb Gallery, Watermill, Long Island, NY; Rhode Island School of Design; Barnard College, New York City; Health Gallery, Atlanta
1978 Kornblee Gallery, New York City
1979 Kornblee Gallery, New York City; Jeff Parsons Gallery, Shelter Island, New York; Fairweather Hardin Gallery, Chicago, Illinois; Finch College, New York City; Montclair Museum, New Jersey
1982 Died, July 23

As a young woman

Esther Peterson

"LOVE IS WANTING THE OTHER PERSON TO GROW"

"I never thought of a career. I certainly never planned to have one. My philosophy was much more to be curious and to let things flow, like a river, flow where your interests take you . . . one thing flows into something else, but it always moved in the direction of my social concerns." While the words could be those of a Hindu mystic, the accent could only be that of a woman who grew up in our West, fast and clear and resonant as a fiddle beating out a square dance. The accent indicates a sense of urgency and activism that the words, divorced from their delivery, do not convey.

The woman speaking is Esther Peterson, who at one time or another has been in the union movement, the women's movement, the Civil Rights movement, and the consumers' movement. They are the words of a woman whose philosophy may have allowed curiosity to be her guide, but they are also the words of a woman who was raised in the Mormon church, where a sense of mission is basic to a whole way of life.

Mrs. Peterson was one of six children born in 1906 to Lars and

Annie Eggersten in Provo, Utah, where her father was superintendent of the schools until his health broke down and he "lightened up" by becoming a seminary teacher for the Mormon church in the small town of Spanish Fork nearby. In keeping with her Danish ancestry, Mrs. Peterson learned that you had to "make your own things" and be self-sufficient. The family had a farm near Brigham Young University, "with a cow that was fresh and chickens that were fertile and where we used to put up our own fruit, make our own bread, weave our own rugs, and preserve our own jam." She never had a "boughten coat" until she was a freshman at college. "Although we were never poor, our household was run on a tight budget and everything we wore was painstakingly cleaned and mended to last for what seemed like forever." By the time she was a senior in college, her father's health had failed, and again he had to "lighten up" from even the teaching of his classes. However, the elders of the church said they would allow Esther to teach for him and if it worked out, he would not lose his salary. So she taught her father's classes as well as completing her senior year at the age of seventeen. It was, she admits, "a very hard year that year."

Esther Peterson's philosophy may have emphasized the importance of letting things flow like a river, but with the training she received from her family and her church, she would never be able to let things just drift. "As children," she says, "we were taught to sing:

'Have I done any good in the world today?
Have I helped anyone in need?
Have I cheered up the sad
And made someone feel glad?
If not, I have failed indeed . . .' "

The Mormon church expected their youth to "go on a mission and spread the word," but Esther's parents gave her the option of going to college. She opted for college, enrolling in Brigham Young University, where she prepared to become a teacher, for teaching and nursing were at that time the only socially acceptable jobs for women. Though she was at the head of her class in psychology and anatomy, "competing with boys who later became M.D.'s," the idea of becoming a doctor simply never entered her mind.

On graduation, she accepted a position teaching physical education, physiology, and English at the Land Grant College in Cedar City, Utah. She remained there for two years before going east to Columbia University Teachers' College where she earned her master's and met Oliver Peterson.

Peterson was a sociology student at Columbia when they met at a Y.M.C.A. gathering on Morningside Heights. "I was fascinated by him from the very beginning," Esther says, "because his ideas were so different. He opened my eyes to things that had never been a part of my life before. He took me around with him to union meetings, he made me see the slums, he made me see the sweatshops, he showed me poverty and want that I had never known existed. We would sit up all night arguing and though he said he loved me, he said he would not change his views because that would be dishonest. And I fell in love with him." Esther Peterson goes on to explain that conservative though her early training may have been, the Mormon church teaches that "you always have to be doing something more than just for yourself," and that it is essential to form an opinion and be able to defend that opinion honestly. And there was no way that she could honestly defend the social conditions that Oliver Peterson was showing her. Another Mormon tenet is that it is not only the thought that counts, but also the action which gives substance to the thought. She was soon to take action.

By 1930, armed with a master's degree, Esther accepted a post as physical education director at the Winsor School outside of Boston. The director of the school at that time was Katherine

Lord who, as Esther describes her, "had a tremendous influence on my life. Oliver was doing graduate work at Harvard, and I was involved in a good deal of volunteer work, being raised in the church and all. In the course of events I met some girls who worked in the sweatshops and got involved in one of their strikes. I talked with Miss Lord about it because I realized that teaching at a private school and being a union organizer could lead to problems. But Miss Lord said that as long as it didn't affect the quality of my teaching I was free to do what I wanted on my own time. She defended me to the trustees by saying that a class such as ours in a society such as ours must do such things. It gave me great courage."

In the 1930s, in the society Miss Lord was referring to, the practice was to give the servants Thursday nights off. On those nights social activity eased off on Beacon Hill, but it rollicked through the lesser orders down in South Boston, especially at the Y.W.C.A. where the newly married Mrs. Peterson conducted gymnastic and current events classes. These evenings were called "industrial nights" and they were attended by, among others, domestic help and the young girls who did piecework for garment manufacturers, making dresses for which they were paid about ten cents each. Given the size of their pay envelopes, which ranged from four to seven dollars a week, there was very little other than the free activities sponsored by the Y that these young girls could afford. Esther Peterson remembers a Thursday evening when none of the garment workers showed up for her classes. When she went around to their homes to find out what had happened, she was shocked by the living conditions she found. "It was the first time I had seen slum homes and industrial homework, and it really tore me apart," she recalls. The workers had stayed home because they had gone on strike, in protest against a change in the design of the dresses they were making. Instead of square pockets, they were now being asked to sew on heart-shaped pockets which took much more time. At ten cents a dress, a pieceworker couldn't afford to provide such frills. That night Esther Peterson became an activist for the first time. She helped the women coin a name for their cause—they called it the "heartbreaker strike"—and they brought a union in and formed a citizens' committee. She says, "It was a great help to us, and this I found was a place where women could be most supportive." Later, she developed a firm belief in women's ability to effect change.

When Mrs. Peterson was asked to help form a labor union for the public school teachers in the Boston area, she realized where her true vocation lay and left the Winsor School to enter the union movement. For the previous six years she and Oliver had been spending their summers at the Bryn Mawr summer school for women workers in industry—she as a recreation director, he as a librarian—in a program that Hilda Worthington Smith, who was formerly dean of Bryn Mawr, had persuaded some alumnae to sponsor. Of course there was a price to pay for associating with women workers. Esther, like Eleanor Roosevelt, was accused of having deserted her class and was even pointed out by some as a Communist. But she had support, too, especially from her husband, "who strengthened and encouraged me because love is wanting the other person to grow. I don't believe it ever occurred to my husband to question my working even when it earned us less than the cost of the household help." And the household expenses would mount as their children started arriving.

Their first child, a daughter, was born in 1938, the same year Joseph Potofsky, then Secretary-Treasurer of the Amalgamated Clothing Workers, offered Mrs. Peterson a position in that union. Three other children, all boys, came over the next eight years. When Oliver's career took them to Washington, Esther became a lobbyist for the A.C.W.U., and would at times take one of the children with her up to Capitol Hill when campaigning on the union's behalf, for, "I could, if necessary, park him in Senator Estes Kefauver's office." The Senator from Tennessee obviously meant it when he kissed babies. It must have been diverting and effective for a young mother to plead the rights of labor before a Congressman, with or without a baby on her lap.

Esther Peterson was the Amalgamated Clothing Workers' Union soft sell. There were times when she could achieve results where others with a more militant approach would have failed, not only because she was less threatening, but also because of her background. Businessmen of the Midwest and South had more in common with her than with her Eastern male counterparts. She remembers going to Uniontown, Pennsylvania, during the Second World War in order to organize a plant where Army uniforms were being made. Previous to this, through the efforts of Sidney Hillman, President of the A.C.W.U., who was an adviser to President Roosevelt's War Production Board, a resolution had been adopted that the uniforms could be made only in a union shop. The manufacturer, who had always been anti-union, now found that he would be unable to get the contract unless he allowed the union into his plant. It came down to a question of whether he loved the contract more than he hated the union. "So I had to go down there and sell the union to these Pennsylvania and Virginia people who were very American, very un-New Yorkerish, and that was quite an experience for me." But she sold it.

In 1948, Oliver was named labor attaché to Sweden, and for the next ten years they lived abroad. Though Esther was not officially working during those years, she did prepare reports on household employment standards in Sweden and the woman's role in bettering working conditions. She also participated in conferences sponsored by the International Federation of Free Trade Unions—an organization of non-Communist workers—so when they returned to Washington she was prepared to reenter the ranks of the labor movement in the Industrial Union of the A.F.L./C.I.O. What she was not prepared for was the unequal pay women were receiving and when she discovered that she was paid less than the man she replaced, she became a crusader for equal pay and also for minimum wage laws. "I had learned," she says, "in my early days that women always got the short end of the stick as far as pay is concerned."

Mrs. Peterson's fight for minimum wage coverage has at times brought her in conflict with the E.R.A. supporters. In 1962, as President Kennedy's Director of the Woman's Bureau, she accused the stalwarts of the E.R.A. movement of being "pains in the neck." "Well, they were, you know," she says, as we sat in front of the fire in her living room one early spring afternoon. "The people who were pushing for E.R.A. would not help us in our work for equal pay or help us get women covered under the Fair Labor Standards Act. They felt the E.R.A. would automatically take care of that. But some legal experts thought we needed to get those laws on the books first, then go for an amendment. We had made a great effort to cover men and women with the minimum wage law, and I did not want to sacrifice that protective legislation by having an amendment to the Constitution that would declare everybody equal because that would mean losing the little bit we had gained, the wage laws that not only protect women but men as well. So when it came up to a vote in the Senate we supported the Hayden rider which said that the E.R.A. was fine as long as it did not upset the legislation already on the books."

Then there was the embarrassing problem of Peterson's position on Title VII of the Civil Rights Act, which the sisterhood was in no mood to forgive and forget for a long time. Title VII stated that there would be no discrimination on the basis of race, color, or creed. When Senator Howard Smith from Virginia, who had long been "the biggest opponent of woman's anything" wanted to add sex to the amendment, Esther was against it. She thought it would kill any chance for the bill's passage "and therefore I did not support it because I did not want to ride equality for women on the backs of my black sisters." The bill passed in any case, and she admits being wrong on that one.

Esther Peterson lives on the outskirts of the capital in a large white Federal-style house with noble columns, the kind of place where George Washington would have liked to have slept. Inside, the walls are covered with photographs of national figures— national Democratic figures—such as Eleanor Roosevelt, Adlai Stevenson, Jack Kennedy, Hubert Humphrey, Lyndon B. Johnson, Paul Douglas, and Jimmy Carter. It is apparent that Peterson is not the "new girl on the block." In fact, she is generally recognized as one of the people who know their way around the crazy quilt of Washington bureaucracy, and whenever a new Democratic administration comes to town her services are in great demand. It was L.B.J. who brought her to the White House as the first Presidential Assistant for Consumer Affairs; when Jimmy Carter came to Washington, he also appointed Mrs. Peterson Special Assistant for Consumer Affairs to lead the Consumer Office, to advise him and "represent the user." There was a nice touch to these appointments for at last she had become a missionary—a missionary to fight the lobbyist, the special interest groups, the "entrenched." It's a role she welcomed because she believes that the "marketplace does not always work in the best interest of the consumer," and about that, she can talk with the fervor of a Joseph Smith or a Brigham Young, but mercifully with humor.

During the years when Nixon and Ford served as Presidents, Mrs. Peterson moved into the private sector and worked as a consumer adviser to the Grant food chain. This was obviously a ticklish business as the consumers might think that she had sold out to industry and the executives of Grant wondered whether she would hamper their creative selling efforts. What neither knew was that Mrs. Peterson had taken the job on the condition that she would have complete freedom to act according to her convictions and the authority to participate in the decision-making process. Also, the president of Grant was anxious to develop a unique program in which the "in-house" consumer advocate's function was to represent the buyer rather than serve as apologist for the seller. What intrigued her about the job was the opportunity to obtain a practical knowledge of the marketplace before going to Congress and requesting protective legislation.

One of the practical things she discovered right away was the "heavy hand of Federal bureaucracy" at work. For example, among the additives that consumers have been concerned about is FD&C Red which is used, in among other things, dye for maraschino cherries. When Grant developed an additive-free product some people at the Food and Drug Administration hailed it as a victory, others voiced concern that the cherries were no longer red, but rather yellow, and prohibited them from bearing the proud name of maraschino. Yet another time Grant attempted to develop a hot dog free of nitrites, which are suspected of being a cancer-producing factor. When they sent a package of their hot dogs over to the U.S. Department of Agriculture for tests of bacterial growth, the official who received them thought they were a gift and promptly took them home and had a cookout.

Nevertheless, Mrs. Peterson made progress in protecting the chain's consumers and Grant made progress in protecting its profits, which continued to remain above the average for the industry. Among the innovations she initiated was unit pricing for comparing the cost of competing products that are sold in varying sizes, dating products in English rather than in code, disclosing ingredients in order of their predominance, and stating the percentage of ingredients contained in combined foods, such as the amount of pork in a can of pork and beans or the amount of beef in a tin of beef stew. If they packaged consciences, Esther Peterson's would be marked "giant-sized."

ESTHER PETERSON

1906   Born Esther Eggersten, Provo, Utah

1927   A.B., Brigham Young University

1927–1929   Teacher, Branch Agricultural College, Center City, Utah

1930   M.A., Columbia Teachers' College

1930–1936   Teacher, Winsor School, Boston

1932–1939   Teacher, Bryn Mawr Summer School for Women Workers in Industry

1932   Married Oliver A. Peterson

1938–1946   Daughter Karen Kristine born (1938) and sons Eric Niels (1939), Iver Echart (1942), and Lars Erling born (1946)

1939–1944   Assistant Director, Amalgamated Clothing Workers of America

1948–1958   To Sweden, where Oliver Peterson was labor attaché

1961–1964   Director, Woman's Bureau, U.S. Department of Labor

1961–1969   Assistant Secretary for Labor Standards

1961–1963   Vice-Chairman, President's Commission on Status of Women

1964–1967   Assistant to the President for Consumer Affairs

Esther and Oliver

1969–1970   Legislative Representative of A.C.W.U.

1970–1977   Consumer Adviser to Grant Food Corporation

1977–1980   Special Assistant to the President for Consumer Affairs

With Eleanor Roosevelt at the Council on Status of Women, Hyde Park

Peterson and her grandchildren, 1980

Aline Porter

"ART
IS A
SHARED
EXPERIENCE"

"Because I gave up painting for ten—no, fifteen—years doesn't mean I had given up being an artist. Far from it, I simply devoted my creative urge to raising our three sons which took a great deal of time and absorbed all my energies."

This fragile woman leans forward as she warms to her subject. "At one point I really had to make a conscious decision whether to be a mother or paint. It was not a difficult decision for me . . . I wanted children. While some can do both, I know other women artists who have also had to make this decision. Many of them stayed with painting—Mary Cassatt, Hedda Sterne, Georgia O'Keeffe, Loren MacIver, and Helen Frankenthaler, to mention a few. As for myself, I can only do one thing well at a time." The things she does one at a time are a testimony to the remarkable qualities of Aline Porter, a Bostonian who now lives and works outside Santa Fe, for the results of her work both as a mother and an artist are impressive.

Aline is married to Dr. Eliot Porter, nature photographer and conservationist, and the history of both their families extends

Eliot Porter

deep into the artistic community of our country. Her mother painted, her brother-in-law, Fairfield Porter, was among our most important twentieth-century painters and critics. Fairfield's wife is a poet, one of the Porters' sons is a sculptor, another son works in wrought-iron and silver, and Eliot's nephew is a print maker. In many ways they are a storybook American family: good-looking, well educated, independent, comfortably off, respected, and inwardly secure. If you were to line them up for a family portrait, the resulting picture would convey the rock-rib character of an eighteenth-century Yankee woodcut.

Aline was born into a New England family that might have come straight from a novel by Henry James. The Kilhams took it as a matter of course that leisurely pilgrimages abroad were a cultural experience that every well-bred Easterner should have from time to time. Her mother was in the habit of returning often to France; her grandmother before her knew and loved the Paris of Mary Cassatt. In the fall of 1918, when she was nine, Aline accompanied her mother, two sisters, and two of her brothers to the City of Lights. It was her first visit to Paris and she fell in love with it. They stayed almost a year, living on the Boulevard St. Michel, where she remembers rolling a hoop beneath the walnut trees in the Luxembourg Gardens across the way. Her mother painted, the children went to school, and for Aline le Bon Dieu was in His heaven.

It was during this period that Aline's mother awakened her interest in painting and eight years later, having been awarded the Nora Saltenstall scholarship from the Winsor School in Boston, she returned to Paris with her mother to study under André l'Hôte, whose classes emphasizing color theory were popular with American students. She arrived two days after Lindberg had landed but, unlike Lindy, she stayed in France for a year, going down to Provence in the summer to paint the countryside Cézanne loved so well.

A number of Americans were studying in Paris during the late

1920s and early '30s, but Aline seems to have shown more talent than most, if the number of exhibitions she had after her return to Boston is any testament. Between the ages of twenty and twenty-six she had four one-woman exhibitions, as well as being included in the Whitney Museum Annual, which at that time had only seventy-one entrants—an unusual accomplishment for such a young woman.

"If I am ever famous," she said one morning as we sat in her kitchen which looks out over the mountains of New Mexico, "it will be for my dollhouses. They tell me that one of the most popular pieces in the Santa Fe museum is the adobe house with all the furniture I made and gave them a few years back." The statement isn't surprising because Aline's dollhouses summarize her two great passions: family and nest building, combined with her love of art. It also takes into account a third characteristic— the respect she has for people who can work beautifully and precisely with their hands. All three of her sons have that ability and she claims that a good measure of the credit belongs to her husband.

All the Porter children are self-reliant. They have had to be, for they've spent much of their youth in the wild. One of their father's books, *In Wildness Is the Preservation of the World*, reflects his own beliefs which have, of course, influenced the attitudes of his boys. Eliot taught bacteriology and biological chemistry at Harvard bewteen 1930 and 1938 before he decided to devote his life to photography. That decision came about when Porter was almost forty years old and Alfred Stieglitz gave him what was to be the last exhibition by a photographer to be held at Porter's New York gallery, An American Place. After that he resigned from teaching and they moved to New Mexico, where their boys grew up.

The move west in 1939 was difficult for Mrs. Porter, who had spent all her life either in the East or abroad. Certainly, when she arrived in Santa Fe it was not love at first sight. However, it was

191

Eliot's choice and that was good enough for her. And there were always the summers to look forward to—those long, happy, isolated months on their island off the coast of Maine with nobody there but the family, the seagulls, and the daily mail boat. To this day the Porters still do not have a telephone in Maine. In summer the island becomes something of a one-family artist colony with Aline painting her flowers, Eliot photographing, son Stephen at work on his wooden totems, and Fairfield, for the many years he was there, working on the oils that captured so well the gentle summer light of Maine.

Aline's flower paintings have some of Redon's mystery, set as they are against a flat background of brilliant or pastel color with no horizon line, creating the impression that they are emerging from a morning mist. They are wonderfully well executed for she combines the old masters' respect for detail with the Impressionists' reverence for light. She is perhaps the only person who grows flowers in order to paint them—in much the same way that Barnett Newman is reported to have said that he paints pictures in order to have something to look at. Not being prolific, she dislikes having to part with her work. The real reason that she allows it to be exhibited at all is not for the potential sale, although it sells off the wall, but because she believes that an artist must not work only for herself. Art for her is a shared experience.

Another area of Mrs. Porter's work are the boxes which contain all manner of found objects and are often compared to those of Joseph Cornell. She objects to this comparison for the simple reason that "he was such a great artist that no one can, or should, be compared with him. He was unique." Also, the comparison is too easy; on closer inspection, the work of these two artists bears little resemblance. The imagery of Aline's boxes is far less somber than Cornell's; hers are generally more open, are day scenes rather than night scenes, and have more objects found in nature than from the city's detritus.

Aline's husband spent many summers collecting birds' eggs from abandoned nests which he gave her to include in some of her boxes. "Eliot knows when a bird has abandoned its nest," she said. That is one thing Aline Porter would not know how to do.

ALINE PORTER

1909 Born Aline Kilham, Brookline, Massachusetts

1918 Traveled to Paris with her family

1927 Awarded scholarship to study painting in Paris for one year. Studied in atelier of André l'Hôte in Paris and in Provence, and at art school in Vienna

1930–1938 Five one-woman shows in Boston

1936 Married Eliot Porter. Moved to Cambridge, Massachusetts. Spent almost all future summers on an island in Penobscot Bay, Maine. Studied painting with Karl Zerbe in Cambridge for six months

1938 Son Jonathan born

1939 Work included in the Whitney Museum of American Art Annual

1941 Son Stephen born

1946 Son Patrick Eliot born

1939–1940 Lived in Santa Fe for one winter

1946 Moved to Santa Fe permanently

1957–1962 One-woman shows at Knopp-Hunter Gallery, Museum of Fine Arts, and Eleanor Bedell Gallery, Santa Fe; Betty Parsons Gallery, New York, and Galleria Escondida, Taos

1963 Participated in group show, Ruins Gallery, Taos—included Agnes Martin, Bee and Louis Ribak

1964 Family show at Manchester Gallery, Taos, with husband Eliot, photographer, and son Stephen, sculptor

1971 Double show, St. John's College, with Eliot Porter

1972–1975 One-woman shows at the Janus Gallery, Santa Fe, paintings and first show of boxes; St. John's College, Santa Fe. Also included in the Christmas Show at the Museum of Fine Arts, Santa Fe, exhibiting boxes; and Betty Parsons Gallery

1977 Group show, "Eleven Women Artists," and one-woman show of paintings and boxes, Elaine Horwitch Gallery, Santa Fe

Porter in her studio

Living room of Sante Fe house

Eliot Porter in his studio

1979 One-woman show, Betty Par-
      sons Gallery
1980 Included in "The Porter
      Family" Exhibition, Parrish
      Art Museum, Southampton,
      New York

Piece *(box of found objects) by Aline Porter*

Anna Rosenberg

"MY FATHER DRILLED INTO ME THAT I MUST SERVE THIS COUNTRY"

If Anna Rosenberg had been given her way, she would have become a professional gardener rather than a labor negotiator and presidential troubleshooter. What she really loves is roses.

Probably the only time she was ever talked into something that she was not keen to do occurred when General George C. Marshall persuaded her to accept the position as Assistant Secretary of Defense in charge of military manpower requirements back in 1950. She had been serving on Senator Stuart Symington's War Production Board at which Marshall had testified on the military needs created by the Korean War; Miss Rosenberg's flat-out approach in dealing with problems must have impressed him as she had impressed President Roosevelt some years before. Marshall had been trying to find someone to accept the post of overseeing military production and had just been turned down by the thirtieth industrialist because he had promised his wife that when he retired he would take her traveling.

" 'Well, I,' said Marshall, 'promised my wife that when I retire we'll see the roses bloom that we planted. . . . We were in so many places. We planted so many roses. . . . We never went back to see them bloom.' He didn't know that I had a mania about roses. I was so touched," she said, "that when he asked me to come down to Washington for three months and help him I couldn't say no." She was there two years and three months. But there was another factor that made it impossible for her to refuse General Marshall's offer. Anna Rosenberg makes George M. Cohan look downright subversive when it comes to patriotism. However, this didn't keep the late Senator Joseph McCarthy from accusing her of being a member of the Communist Party—a comrade—and infiltrating the Pentagon. During her confirmation hearings, to prove it, he produced a witness to her alleged affiliations. (The witness was given to such paranoia that he once sued Cardinal Spellman for not letting him join the Catholic church.) Anyway, the F.B.I. found the right Anna Rosenberg and "the whole unpleasant affair came to an end." In her office there is a picture of Anna Rosenberg at the front lines in Korea just one year later, inspecting a twenty-four-inch shell with her name inscribed upon it—a shell soon to be fired toward the "comrades."

The irony does not strike her as anything out of the ordinary, because most of her eighty years have been made up of just such curious vignettes. In fact, the first of a series of bizarre events that were directly to affect her life was caused by the last reigning Hapsburg, Franz Joseph, some few years before fate sent his great-nephew and the heir apparent, Francis Ferdinand, down to Sarajevo against all good advice. Her father was in the furniture business and had been made supplier to the royal family very much in the English manner of a supplier to the king or queen. Franz Joseph summoned her father, Albert Lederer, to Schoenbrunn Palace one fine morning and said that he wanted to replace the furniture in all his residences with French antiques and would Herr Lederer please attend to the details. Her father scoured Europe and brought back to Budapest the most marvelous array of of Louis XIV baroque and Louis XV rococo *meubles,* and the emperor was delighted. Delighted but capricious, for Franz Joseph then changed his mind and so Herr Lederer was stuck with a warehouse full of French antiques and a war coming.

That's when he came to America. Anna, her mother, and sister followed three years later. "My father was a man who couldn't make a beginning in Hungary and he made one here. He was such an enthusiastic patriot. My father drilled into me that I must serve this country, and that attitude of great love you couldn't help but assimilate."

Anna Rosenberg is a compact woman of 5 foot 4 inches. Her movements are rapid, staccato, crisp, and efficient, like a surgeon operating—a lot of movement, but no wasted motion. She cannot weigh a hundred pounds, but there is a kind of energy that pulses out from her. When you shake hands with her you feel you should ground yourself to avoid an electrical shock.

When Rosenberg was a student at Wadleigh High School in New York City she plugged that current into her first cause: a student strike because "we didn't have enough school facilities and had to go there in shifts. I went from four to eight P.M., and we sat two in a seat." Incensed over the injustice of the situation, Anna marched a group of students down to the Board of Estimate to plead their case. "You could see those aldermen smoking cigars, not listening at all. One of them got bored and started to yawn, and then they all began to leave the hall." She remembers calling after them, " 'Very well, gentlemen, you may have heard enough, but now you will hear from our parents who are your constituents.' And this fat alderman said, 'All right, little girl, now tell us what you want.' As if we hadn't told it all before." So she restated her case and the next year Wadleigh students each had a desk and no split shifts. "That was my first political experience," Anna says. She was fourteen.

While this may have been Mrs. Rosenberg's first political experience and her first brush with bargaining, it did not evidence the method she would employ later on in settling labor disputes: that would be humor and uncommon solutions derived from clear observation of the facts. She learned the wisdom of these methods during the First World War when she and her sister volunteered to serve as student nurses in an Army hospital. They were assigned to the Recreation Department, and it was her job to telephone people and ask them to invite the soldiers to dinner or the theater. Within a week she had made two observations: that the people would always take the soldiers to a restaurant, and that "they only wanted boys on crutches . . . to show how patriotic they were. If we couldn't place the boys, we'd say, 'All right, go get some crutches upstairs.' And I used to say to them before they'd leave, 'Don't forget to lean on those crutches.' "

One of the soldiers was Julius Rosenberg, whom she would marry in 1919, just before he left for Europe. While Anna's husband was not wounded, he returned from the war riddled with ulcers, suffering from various nervous disorders, and in no condition to support his wife and baby son. Out of necessity, Anna went to her friend, Mrs. Henry Moskowitz, who performed public relations chores for, among others, Alfred E. Smith, then the Governor of New York State. When Anna offered to learn the business by working for nothing, Mrs. Moskowitz's advice was "If you ask for nothing, your services are worth nothing." Fortunatley, that was a piece of wisdom that Anna would often honor in the breach, for years later when she became Roosevelt's Secretary to the War Labor Board, she refused to accept a salary. Perhaps she did not consider arbitrating labor disputes as a mainstream activity because she remarked, "I never did labor negotiations professionally—I never took money for it." Be that as it may, Mayors La Guardia and Wagner constantly called on her to help settle labor disputes in New York City, and Franklin Delano Roosevelt appointed her to the National Labor Relations Board in 1930. (N.L.R.B. is the agency charged with negotiating labor complaints, minimum-wage agreements, and the standards governing the conduct between labor and management.)

What Mrs. Rosenberg brought to negotiations was a sense of humor that helped unglue some of the positions that had become calcified by endless debate. She remembers one instance when all the breweries in New York and New Jersey had been out on strike for ten weeks. She was called in by the Rheingold Beer Company to see if an agreement could be reached. "The brewery unions met at the old Piccadilly Hotel. Philip Sipser, a leading labor lawyer, represented the unions and after talking a couple of hours, he turned to me and said, 'Now look here, Anna, I know these men, I spend my time with them, I work with them, I play with them, I eat with them, I sleep with them . . .' and I stopped him and said, 'Phil, you got me there.' That broke the tension, and they started to laugh; they thought it was great. You know, I had no trouble after that." Later she settled three transit strikes in New York City and remembers spending those New Year's Eves in City Hall with Michael Quill, head of the Transit Workers' Union, because if they left one minute before the midnight deadline, his union would think he sold out. "Relax, Anna," Quill used to say, "sit down, let's spend another New Year's Eve in City Hall."

It is immediately apparent that one of the things Anna Rosenberg enjoys least is sitting back and relaxing once the job has been accomplished. Like an automobile's batteries, hers are recharged by running at full speed, not sitting in the garage. It was only while she was on the job negotiating labor disputes that she could sit day and night with Michael Quill or John L. Lewis, of the United Mine Workers' Union, or James Hoffa of the Teamsters' Union and match them cup for black cup of "java," until the dispute was settled. In fact her practice was to keep these men locked in a room for, as she says, "When the negotiators go back to their union halls, they come back full of pep and new demands."

But for all their differences, every labor man called Mrs. Rosenberg "Anna," something that her mother found shocking.

"My mother was a very educated, cultured woman. She didn't approve of me dealing with the teamsters. I'll never forget one day when we were walking along the street, a truck came along and the driver leaned out and yelled, 'Hi, Anna. How ya doin'?' Mother looked at me aghast and said, 'Those are your acquaintances?' " Yes, those were her acquaintances along with the mayors of New York City, the captains of industry, the leaders of Congress, and the next five Presidents of the United States who would also call her Anna. She once said that the reason that she was an effective labor negotiator was that she loved people.

During the Second World War, when President Roosevelt needed someone to resolve labor disputes, he formed a group of C.I.O. people, headed by Philip Murray and of A.F. of L. people, led by Bill Green. A few years before, in 1937, the labor movement had come apart at the seams when ten unions, including John L. Lewis's powerful U.M.W. and David Dubinsky's I.L.G.W.U., had split from the parent A.F. of L. because of what they considered conservative policies in regard to mass-production industries. "During the war," Mrs. Rosenberg says, "a lot of problems had to be resolved. There were no strikes, but there was friction between unions as well as between labor and management relating to working conditions, wages, and living practices that had to be dealt with." Roosevelt knew that only someone who loved people could bring all these factions to common solutions, and he said, "Anna, you will have to be secretary." And he told Murray and Green, "If you have any problems, call up Anna." Anna the troubleshooter.

The job description for a troubleshooter must be left rather general in order to be most effective. It would have made no difference if they had made up a chart of responsibilities as long as Queen Victoria's genealogy table for when it came to bringing pressure to bear, the only thing that counted was her friendship with the President. Roosevelt knew this and some of the appointments in addition to those connected with the Labor Board may have set a record for vagueness. But while they may have been vague, they were inspirational because F.D.R. seems to have been particularly adept at looking over the horizon. He looked over one horizon in 1944 and saw the end of the war with the problems that would arise at its conclusion, assuming an Allied victory. So he sent Anna over to have a look around Europe. No specific assignment, no particular title, no time limit or travel restrictions, although it is doubtful that he would have approved of her landing as she did on Omaha Beach on D-Day plus 2. "Just come back and tell me what you think the boys need, what they ought to have there, what they should have when they come back, and what they are interested in."

Well, what she found fascinated her, for she discovered that most of the G.I.'s were worried that the men who had stayed home were continuing to receive an education, which would give them a decided advantage when peace was restored. Most of them had never finished school, never wanted to, and now suddenly they wanted an education. "When I came back and told this to the President he became very excited and said, 'Get together with Samuel Rosenman' [the Budget Director and a lawyer], and then he explained to me what he wanted." What she had given him was the idea for the G.I. Bill of Rights.

The measure of Anna Rosenberg's intelligence is summed up in her remark that "Roosevelt never gave you precise assignments but he wanted you to come back with precise answers." A measure of the impression she made on her contemporaries is that a year later, in 1945, General Eisenhower asked President Truman to send Anna to Europe again so that she could continue to observe and advise. The same year Eisenhower recommended that she be awarded the Medal of Freedom for her work with the troops. Today it hangs in her office, along with the Medal of Merit awarded by Truman for her work in the Pentagon as Assistant Secretary of Defense. It was during this period that she became close to Mrs. Eleanor Roosevelt, the President's widow. "I admired her greatly and Adlai Stevenson was so right when he characterized her as a woman who would rather light candles than curse the darkness."

The two men Rosenberg admires the most are Paul Hoffman, at one time director of the Marshall Plan and who she later married, and the man for whom the plan was named, George Catlett Marshall, the great soldier-statesman—and rose lover. It was Marshall who brought her into the Department of Defense and who sent her on fact-finding missions to Korea, the Turkish-Russian border, Saudi Arabia, and a dozen other places where concerns were rockets not roses. Mrs. Rosenberg has some fascinating scrapbooks filled with pictures of these journeys. I remember one in particular that shows her standing, in her fatigues and parachute boots, talking to towering military men who in an earlier time would have been members of Caesar's Praetorian guard. Even in the snapshots one feels the sense of energy that makes her always the center of the picture no matter where she is standing. These pictures reveal something else: a sense of concentration from which all outside static has been eliminated, whether she is listening to a general or a G.I. Her little electromagnetic field of highly charged particles receives with the same energy that it sends.

ANNA
ROSENBERG

Rosenberg with General Patton, European Theater, 1944

1902 Born Anna Lederer, Budapest, Hungary
1912 Came to the United States
1919 Married Julius Rosenberg
1920 Son Thomas born
1934–1939 Assistant, New York Regional Director National Recovery Administration
1935 Regional Director, National Recovery Administration
1936–1943 Regional Director, Social Security Administration
1941–1942 Office of Defense, Health and Welfare Services
1942–1945 Regional Director, War Manpower Commission
1945 Served as personal representative of Presidents Roosevelt and Truman to the European theater of war to report on problems of returning soldiers
Senior partner, Anna M. Rosenberg Associates, Public and Management Relations Consultant
1950 Assistant Secretary of Defense
1962 Divorced Julius Rosenberg Married Paul Hoffman
1974 Paul Hoffman died
1983 Died, May 9

Rosenberg with American troops in European Theater, 1944

Receiving medal of merit from Secretary of War, Robert P. Patterson

With Generals Jenkins and Van Fleet, questioning Chinese prisoner, Korea, 1952

With Captain Eberle, followed by General Williams, Korea, 1952

Diana Vreeland

"THE WIZARD OF AHS"

There is a story that at one of those office luncheons that Diana Vreeland used to have while Editor-in-Chief of *Vogue,* a new secretary had the temerity to place two slices of white bread beside her bowl of consommé. "Who is responsible for this unintegrated farina?" demanded the high priestess of fashion. When the offender was brought forward, Mrs. Vreeland gently took her hand and said, "Ah, my child, don't you know that people who eat white bread have no dreams?" Dreams are to Vreeland what coal is to heat, yeast is to bourbon, or rain is to spring; that is to say, they are her agents for change. Dreams to her are something that should not be wasted or underrated, but employed in a practical manner. The dreams are the real thing; it is her life that is a fantasy.

One of the advantages Vreeland had was a set of parents who put no stock in formal education, so that fantasy and enthusiasm were never squeezed out of her. Those tedious classroom drills where the rest of us conjugated verbs, memorized prepositions, and recited dates were not to stifle her. In fact, the only school

Augustus John

she remembers is one on Staten Island called Dongan Hall, which her parents had seen advertised in *The New York Times* and to which they promptly dispatched her without bothering to first take the ferry ride themselves. Her mother had to find a school for her sixteen-year-old daughter quickly, as she was off to South Africa for the winter. Later, there was Miss Randall McKeever's, but for the most part the underpinnings of her education rested on the unusual life-style of her parents.

Her mother was an American who spent most of her life in France and her father, Frederick Y. Dalziel, was a Scots banker who lived in Paris, where Diana was born. They lived on the Avenue Foch with a flock of servants and two nannies, one named Pink, who was Diana's own personal nanny and a second, presumably with a more commonplace name, who looked after the younger sister. Their summers were spent in either Deauville or Venice. That is, they were spent in Deauville until her mother's maid burned down one wing of the just completed Normandy Hotel while pressing Mommy's tea gown one sunny afternoon. After that, they went to Venice until the cholera epidemic, about which Thomas Mann wrote in *Death in Venice*, forced them to come to the States. But apart from the influence of traveling, it was the people their parents chose to travel with that influenced Diana most.

The Dalziels' house on the Avenue Foch was a gathering place for the Russian Corps de Ballet, which during that period (1910–1911), included Diaghilev and Nijinsky "who would sit in the corner like a funny pug dog," together with Ira Rubinstein and the great Russian operatic basso, Chaliapin. Since Diana was only five or six at the time, the combination of a stuffy French governess and the presence of these high-voltage Russians and their almost paranoic demand for perfection may shed some light on her respect for manners (drilled in by Pink) and her regard for high standards (insisted on by Diaghilev). But she denies this, saying that her respect for manners and high standards stems from being 50 percent British.

It is partly because of this and partly because her parents seemed to enjoy being where the action was, that Diana and her baby sister were taken to the coronation of George V in 1911. "Ah, that was where my family was great . . . we never missed anything, and that is why I have grown up with a total sense of vision. . . . Get the point?" She is indeed a completely visually oriented person and, as she says, like El Greco ("God knows I am not comparing myself to El Greco"), she suffers from a slight astigmatism. She adds that she was frightfully shy before becoming slightly blind, but in losing some sight she gained in confidence. Lack of confidence is not Vreeland's short suit today, yet as a child she remembers wishing, like Topper in the old movies, that she could make herself invisible.

In April 1914, when her parents arrived in this country and shipped the two children (aged about four and eight) out to Southampton to spend the summer with their American grandmother, it probably didn't help that neither spoke English. Nor did it help that, rather than going to school when the family returned to New York, Diana was sent to study ballet with Fokine, "the only imperial ballet master who ever left Russia." She is quoted as saying that she was "very, very poor at it." She is also quoted as saying that Fokine was "a brute." It also probably did not help that about the time she was getting used to our American ways in the East an epidemic of infantile paralysis broke out, and she and her sister were shipped out to Cody, Wyoming. Her unorthodox childhood, if not the cause of her shyness, was certainly no cure for it.

Cody, Wyoming, in 1916 was not the Paris of Gigi which up to then the children had known best, but they seem to have managed, for Wild Bill Cody took a fancy to these two small French-speaking children, gave them each a pony and taught them how to ride. He was more fun than Fokine by a country mile.

For the next six years the Dalziels continued to live in New York, where Diana's father worked in a brokerage firm. Her mother, having fallen in love with Wyoming, divided much of her time between it and Scotland, where they went shooting each August. Diana remembers being frightfully lonely in both places. She also remembers, with particular distaste, having to go to Inverness in 1923 for she had fallen in love with an American she had met in Saratoga the previous summer, and the last thing she wanted was to spend August walking through the rain to the post office to collect his letters. His name was Reed Vreeland, and she knew he was serious, because, crossing on the *Cameronia*, there had been a cable saying he missed her and loved her. They were married the following March in St. Thomas's Church on Fifth Avenue.

Diana was well into her thirties before she ever seriously considered putting her love of clothes and fashion to professional use. But even when she was very young she would, according to people who knew her, dress in a style that was unique and use cosmetics in a way that was a "bit much." Not all women understood her way of dressing, and when she moved to Albany with her husband the only person who really appreciated her originality was Mrs. Lilly Van Renssalaer, the town matriarch. "Ah, Albany," Mrs. Vreeland recalls, "a beautiful old Dutch town with men in shiny shoes and bright minds to match." The Vreelands' two sons were born there. "Bringing up sons is such a pleasure . . . I wouldn't have known what to do about daughters," admits the woman who has probably introduced more daughters to fashion than any other American. But the family was not to live there long, as Reed had taken a job in London in 1929, just before the crash.

If the traveling Diana did during her childhood was a substitute for school, the next eight years in London were to be her college. She read a great deal, traveled on the Continent in the summer and along with her friend Edwina d'Erlanger, opened a lingerie shop in Berkley Square. "That was the thing to do then —Syrie Maugham had one, Sybil Colefax had one, Kay Norton had one, and we had one. . . . Get the point?"

Running a shop may have been the thing to do, but hardly the kind of demanding work that Vreeland came to thrive on years later when she went to work as the American Fashion Editor of *Harper's Bazaar*. The way in which she secured the job on *Bazaar* must go down in the annals of American labor as one of the most eccentric exercises in hiring practices ever recorded. Carmel Snow, the *Bazaar*'s Editor-in-Chief, spotted Diana dancing one night at the St. Regis roof, telephoned her the next day and asked if she'd ever thought of working in fashion. "Lord, no, never . . . I've never even been in an office before . . ." "Are you responsible?" Mrs. Snow asked her. "Ah, not really, I have two sons and lots of people to help me, and I rarely rise before noon." Carmel Snow did not believe her, perhaps because Vreeland had already contributed to some of the "Why Don't You" columns for *Bazaar*, which made suggestions that ricocheted from the practical to the hilarious. ("Why don't you rinse your child's head in dead champagne to keep it golden," "Why don't you have a white monkey fur bedcover mounted on yellow velvet?" etc.). Also, Mrs. Snow recognized talent when she saw it.

That was 1939, and for the next quarter of a century Diana Vreeland, Art Director Alexey Brodovitch, and Carmel Snow turned out one of the most engaging and successful magazines ever published. Vreeland is modest about her own contribution, saying that a lion's share of the credit must go to Brodovitch and Snow, but the *Bazaar* was a fashion magazine and she was its Fashion Editor. Her taste was on the line month after month, out front there like a point man reconnoitering the terrain. Her terrain was Seventh Avenue, and she was the first to uncover its assets. She was the first to recognize that the Nettie Rosensteins, the Jane Rothenbergs, the Claire McCardells, and Hattie Carnegies had a talent far in excess of their reputation. She was the first to affirm that while French designers were doing marvelous work, so were the Americans. She could do this not only because she believed in American fashion but because she had spent most of her life up to then in Europe and could justify the comparison. She could do it because she was always a little ahead of her time and had the ability to see around corners. She could do it because no one would ever accuse Diana Vreeland of being afraid of luxury, and if she thought Seventh Avenue could produce luxury, her conviction was pretty strong evidence. She could do it because like Diaghilev "she stressed innovation rather than nostalgia for past glories."

In the 1960s, during her ten years as Editor-in-Chief at *Vogue*, her disregard for "past glories" dovetailed with the fresh innovative upsurge of the era. She launched more models (Marisa Berenson, Jane Holzer, Penelope Tree, Lauren Hutton, and Verushka, among others) and experimented with more new photographers (Maurice Hogenboom, David Bailey, Patrick Lichfield, Claude Picasso, David Massey, Jack Robinson, Gianni Penati, Raymundo de Larrain, and Arnaud de Rosnay) than any fashion editor before her. She not only wanted but needed new talent, for she was sending the old masters like Irving Penn, Richard Avedon, Henry Clarke, Horst P. Horst, and Tony Snowdon around the world as if she were a dispatcher in a messenger service. Avedon was sent to Paris, Ireland, Japan; Clarke to Syria, Jordan, India; Penn to Nepal, Cameroon, New Guinea; Horst to Europe and North Africa, and Snowdon to the New York Aquarium to photograph white whales and to Maryland to photograph white stallions. Vreeland apparently took it seriously when someone told her that the jet was a common carrier.

But of all of her accomplishments it will probably be her work as special consultant to the Costume Institute of the Metropolitan Museum of Art in Manhattan for which she will be remembered longest. According to Truman Capote, "She walked into that cellar that didn't have three visitors a day and look what she has done." What she has done over ten years of her consultancy is to plan and have mounted ten annual exhibitions that together have attracted over four million visitors. The exhibitions have ranged from romantic and glamorous Hollywood designs to fashions of the Hapsburg era where the men, according to an article in *Vogue* by the English writer John Richardson, "were never at war, but always dressed for it." She curtsied to her mother's old friend Diaghilev by showing the costumes and designs of the Ballet Russe and bowed to Balenciaga by acknowledging his mastery in her first exhibition.

All this because she knows how to translate dreams to reality and never eats white bread.

DIANA
VREELAND

In Arizona, 1942

Costumes from "Fashions of the Hapsbu Era" at the Metropolitan Museum, 197

1906 Born Diana Dalziel, Paris, France
1911 To coronation of George V with her parents
1914 To the States with her parents
1916 Traveled to Cody, Wyoming, with her sister
1924 Married Thomas Reed Vreeland
1924–1928 Lived in Albany, New York
1925 Son Thomas Reed born
1928 Son Frederick D. born
1929 Moved to London
1936 Returned to New York
1936–1938 Wrote "Why Don't You" column for **Harper's Bazaar**
1939–1962 Fashion Editor of **Harper's Bazaar**
1962–1971 Editor-in-Chief of **Vogue**
1966 Thomas Reed Vreeland died
1971–Present Consultant to the Costume Institute of the Metropolitan Museum of Art, New York City
1972 Awarded Legion d'Honneur
1972–1982 Exhibitions at the Costume Institute: "World of Balenciaga"; "The Tens, The Twenties, The Thirties: Inventive Clothes 1909–39"; "Romantic and Glamorous Hollywood Design"; "American Women of Style"; "The Glory of the Russian Costume"; "Vanity Fair: Treasure Trove of the Costume Institute"; "Diaghilev, Costumes and Designs of the Ballet Russes"; "Fashions of the Hapsburg Era, Austria, Hungary"; "The Manchu Dragon: Costumes of China; The Ch'ing Dynasty"; and "The Eighteenth-Century Woman"

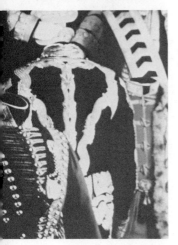

Vreeland, by Christian Berard

Vreeland, 1979, in front of Bill Acton's 1932 portrait of her

Illustration from Vreeland's column, "Why don't you?", **Harpers Bazaar,** *1937*

Clarabelle Williams

"IF
WE REACH,
WE SHALL ACCOMPLISH"

Before the Civil War, plantation owners had what they called
jackleg preachers, black men who would go through the slave
quarters and preach the Gospel or at least that portion of the
Gospel that their masters found convenient for keeping the
peace. They would preach that children should obey their parents and servants should obey their masters, the implication
being that blacks, who fell into both categories, had a double
responsibility to remain obedient if they ever hoped to get into
a separate but equal heaven. Clarabelle Williams's grandfather,
Steven Drisdale, was just such a preacher. As a child, he had been
captured off the coast of Africa, sold to an Alabama family and
somewhat later resold to Buck and Judy Drisdale, slave owners
living on a farm near La Grange, Fayette County, Texas. As was
the custom of many slaves, he adopted the name of the family he
served and as was the custom of many slave owners, Steven was
married off to a female slave named Maria Drisdale by having the
two of them jump over a broomstick; a ritual that substituted for
both the civil ceremony and the church vows.

Whatever the qualifications required to serve as a jackleg preacher, ambition was not included as part of the job description. After the Civil War the very qualities that made Steven Drisdale a model slave weren't helpful to free man, so Maria left him for another because she didn't want "to live with a man who just preached and wouldn't work."

By then she had three sons, one of whom, Isaac, was to become Clara's father. Maria, her sons and new husband Peyton Washington began farming as sharecroppers on part of the Drisdale land, later managing to buy a hundred acres of it. It was here that Clara, her two brothers and two sisters were born and raised along with a "whole pack" of cousins. Over a century later, up 'until this day, members of her family own and work the same spread.

Clara remembers the shanty in which they lived, surrounded by fields that came right up to the door, where scrawny wire-haired dogs with long tails and pointed muzzles scratched for fleas and how, after it rained, you could stand knee-deep in mud and still get dust blown in your eyes. She remembers chopping cotton, planting potatoes, gathering beans, and harvesting corn, but above all, she remembers how her father taught himself to read from an old blue-backed spelling book, how Mama learned her ABC's from a cast-off primer and how determined they both were to see that their children got an education. "Neither my parents, nor my preacher grandfather had ever attended school for more than two weeks," so in learning to read she became the pride of her grandfather who would bounce her on his knee and boast that "this is going to be my little schoolteacher."

What saved Clara from a life of chopping cotton, tending greens, and hoeing yams was a Texas law enabling each state senator to appoint two black students from his area to black schools. Back in 1901, she was brought to the attention of the Honorable D. A. Paulus, Senator from La Grange Township, Fayette County, Texas. "I was sixteen at the time and there was no high school near the farm, but I got awarded a four-year scholarship to the Prairie View State Normal and Industrial College (actually a high school with two years of college work). You had to be willing to work in the laundry as I did for four whole years helping press men's shirts, wash clothes, and iron sheets, or you had to wait the table or perform some other duty which together with your scholarship and ten dollars a month extra, covered your board. The tuition itself was free." Senator Paulus didn't have to fret over that appointment for Clara became in 1905 the valedictorian of her class of forty-nine students, which was how she qualified to be a teacher "in any colored school in Texas . . . I mean any black school in Texas." To this day she says Negroes, sometimes correcting herself to say black.

When Clarabelle Williams speaks, she speaks rapidly, her small frame leaning forward for emphasis and back to view the effect on her listener. When, on occasion, she gently takes your wrist in her hand to drive home a point it is as if the sound of her words vibrates through her fingertips. Charismatic is an overused word, but for Clara it could have been minted, for there is a strong center about her person that attracts others. One senses that this is a natural leader, a woman who if born a generation or two later could have been a formidable force in the Civil Rights movement.

Back in 1905 nobody bothered to look any deeper than a plow furrow under the ocher-colored dusty fields of Texas. The ranchers still drove their cattle to market; the towns still had wooden sidewalks and unpaved streets; the only thing that came from wells was water; and the schools were one-room frame structures with a flagpole outside and, on the inside, some benches and a teacher's desk, raised on a six-inch platform before a blackboard. It was just such a school in Cameron, Texas, at which Clara first taught for the magnificent sum of $30 a month. Two evenings a week she would help supplement her income by teaching home economics to the local women, who would gather at her house to discuss cooking, sewing, the proper care of children, and probably how to keep their men in line—although this was not part of the curriculum as advertised. For this she took in $15 a month.

It was during this period that she met Jasper Williams, who was teaching school about ten miles south of Cameron. They were introduced by Williams' old teacher, who jokingly presented Jasper as Clara's future husband. She fell in love with him almost immediately. But as Clara explains, "We couldn't get married right away because of his promise to send his brothers and sisters to college." It was not until a decade later that the last of Jasper's ten brothers and sisters earned a sheepskin, so Clara's patience almost matches that of Penelope. All during those ten years they faithfully wrote each other once a month, whether Clara was teaching in Cameron or later in Austin, Texas, or attending summer school in Chicago, which she did in the summer of 1912 or the State School of Methods, which she did almost every other summer.

There is a picture in Clara's house of a man with an intensely sensitive face and eyes that burn out from an oval skull with the passion associated with the prophets. He is wearing a wing collar, cravat, and cutaway coat; the pose speaks of a disposition coiled and ready to spit in the eye of injustice whether real or imagined and a character that will one day be broken because of an inability to bend. It is Jasper Williams's wedding picture, taken on January 21, 1917.

In the following year their first son, Jasper, was born, and America became engaged in the war "over there." An acquaintance of the Williamses—a pharmacist who had been called into service—offered to sell them his small drugstore. They bought it on "our little savings . . . we didn't have much, but we bought it anyway." Clara remembers that at the time it was always referred to as "the Negro drugstore" until they changed the name to the Williams Drugstore. They had a soda fountain with stand-up wire chairs, a whole lot of patent medicine, and a registered pharmacist who was required to mix prescriptions. The next year they had a second son, James, and four years later a third son, Charles. Clara was thirty-eight years of age and Jasper fifty when Charles was born, and if bad luck had dogged them in the past, it was only the preseason warmup to what was coming. Now in speaking of her youngest son's birth she says, "When the baby came out the nurse gasped 'Oh' and covered him up. I was hurting so I didn't think anything of it, but that night I looked down into the little bed where the baby had kicked the covers off, and I saw his crooked little feet with all the toes stuck together. He was kicking and flopping his feet." Clara cuffs her hands to imitate the sound, which is like holding two fish by the tails and smacking them together. Charles had been born with two clubfeet. "I never cried so much in my life. . . . I asked the Lord, why me?" The answer came years later. But then again maybe it came right away because as she says, "His misfortune solidified the family; we decided to work together . . . to see that he got the best education and then as he grew up we would know that his brain was not crippled, too. Oh! We would never have thought of putting him in a garbage can like you read some others do." Instead they put him in school and kept him there summer and winter until he became the first Williams to become a doctor of medicine.

By 1924 Jasper and Clara had been running the drugstore for almost six years, and what they didn't know about the business in the beginning, they had learned and in learning had achieved a modicum of security . . . or thought so. Jasper Williams had many of the qualities that a quarter of a century later Civil Rights leaders would stress as important for the others of black race to emphasize, such as pride in their blackness, recognition of their contributions to this country, rejection of a slave mentality, and a need to redefine their esthetic sensibilities so as to recognize that black is indeed beautiful. However, Jasper Williams was ahead of his time and it is always dangerous to be a point man. One day in 1924 when the insurance agent came around to have the policy signed, Jasper noticed that the premiums had been increased. He commented that the value of the business had not changed radically within the year. The insurance representative, who can hardly be accused of being a good salesman, responded that Jasper didn't have "any right to be thinking about it," didn't have any right to know what the business was worth, and told him "this is your new policy, and I want you to sign it." Take it or leave it. Mr. Williams chose to leave it and no doubt his pride required him to clarify his reason with some rather colorful language. In any case, the agent left without renewing the policy and one month later the place burned to the ground. To this day, Clara Williams is convinced that arson was committed.

About this time, the Elephant Butte Dam on the Rio Grande River designed to help irrigate the land around Las Cruces, New Mexico, was finished. The attraction of good land induced many Southern whites to migrate to Las Cruces, taking along with them black farm laborers. Although the New Mexican schools did not segregate the races, the tradition of the Southern families who settled in the area still required segregated schools and black teachers like Clara were in demand for the newly formed Negro schools. But tradition, like some Spanish wines, often doesn't travel well and as Clara says, "The Negroes didn't want their children hauled around in buses like people don't want it now . . . and the Negroes didn't want separate schools." Also, as the black community was spread over an area of thirty miles up and down the Rio Grande, the school in Las Cruces (where the Williamses settled) was simply too far away for most black children to attend. During the first four months Clara had only five students, two of whom were her own sons, Jasper and James. The authorities recognized almost immediately that what they had created was probably not only the highest teacher to student ratio in the state, if not in the nation, but that no blacks, with the exception of the teacher's children and three others, were receiving any education. Clara was in effect being paid, in large measure, to teach her own sons. To remedy this injustice she was sent thirty miles south to a town named Vado in the heart of the black community, where she taught for one year before returning to Las Cruces and the primary school where her husband was teaching. That same year, Williams ran afoul of the school superintendent on the question of keeping the school open on Lincoln's birthday. The board had decided that the children had already missed one day of school and they should make it up on the holiday. But Mr. Williams decided otherwise. "Anyway," Clara goes on with the story, "Lincoln's birthday comes around and so does the superintendent in his old Model T and asks Jasper where are all the children he's supposed to be teaching. And Mr. Williams cursed him out and said he wasn't teaching anybody on Lincoln's birthday." After that, Williams was effectively banned from ever getting another teaching position in the state.

If Jasper had good reason to suspect the motives of the white community it becomes clear in talking to Clara that she is forgiving of the discrimination she has suffered. She says of the Drisdale family who owned her grandfather, that "they were good people who shared their God and their play. On Sunday they'd go to church, then have picnics where the mothers pooled potluck dinners; we children played hide 'n' seek and everybody sang." And when she was teaching that first year in Las Cruces, it was a "good white man that brought those three little Negro boys who lived on his place to my school." And later it was "some good white friends like we always have had who told us how the superintendent had badmouthed Mr. Williams all over the state so that he decided to give up teaching and put in a claim for a homestead." This kind of response must be placed in context with the less noble acts she witnessed in order to measure the quality of her magnanimity.

For example, in 1937 when she was fifty-one years of age, the first black to enter and subsequently graduate with honors from the New Mexico College of Agriculture and Mechanical Arts, her class members, who had right along refused to sit next to her in lectures, boycotted the graduation ceremony because they didn't want to march in the commencement exercises with a black. The college officials told her that it would save them money if they skipped the march and passed the diplomas out through a window, which is what they did. She prefers, however, to remember that forty years later, acknowledged as an outstanding alumna, she went back to the same college to receive an Honorary Doctor of Laws degree and stood before an audience which gave her a standing ovation and that subsequently a campus street was named in her honor.

The acceptance speech she gave to her alma mater which brought the audience to its feet dealt with the importance of having positive convictions. These, she believes, are what fortified her during the difficult years she spent as the first black woman to enter the now renamed New Mexico State University. "There is," she says, "no alternative to optimism. The only chance we have is to prepare ourselves so that we can go as far as possible. Otherwise, we have only betrayed the precious breath the Lord has given us . . . if we reach we shall accomplish."

The day in 1928 when Jasper Williams went down to the Federal Building in Las Cruces to put in a claim for his 640-acre homestead, the family needed all the optimism that they could muster. They had three children, one of whom was crippled, Jasper was out of work and blacklisted, and Clara, the only breadwinner, was earning $110 a month. The homestead he acquired was seven miles northeast of Las Cruces on the Jornado Road, which today leads on to the forest preserve of the New Mexico State Agricultural College. The area has been described as a desert with mosquitoes. "The land was good if it rained; we planted corn, beans, feed for livestock, and cotton. At times we harvested as much as two bales of cotton in one year," Clara says with obvious pride. Her account of those homesteading years sounds like a black version of the Swiss Family Robinson. "Mr.

Williams, with a helper [whom Clara paid for out of her salary], cut and burned the brush, he cleared the fields, he built a house, strung the barb-wire fences, planted crops, raised some chickens, hogs and a cow, had a horse and mule and later bought a used pickup truck and then a tractor—a secondhand John Deere tractor that the children learned to drive." The boys recall it as a wonderful time of trapping rabbits, hunting birds, killing rattlesnakes, and chasing cayotes.

In 1938, when Charles was fifteen years old, he was taken by a country doctor to the Carrie Tingley Crippled Children's Hospital in a town with the unlikely name of Truth or Consequences, New Mexico, to have an operation on his clubfeet. Whether it was at this time or earlier that Charles decided to study medicine ("to see if I can make all the crippled folks not be crippled anymore") is not clear, but what is clear is that his own handicap was the agent that would bring changes to the Williams family that would alter their lives for generations. At the incredibly young age of twenty-three years, he became the first in a series of doctors in the Williams family that today include Clara's three sons, two grandsons, and two more grandsons attending medical schools.

The youngest, Charles, led the family into medicine in 1946, his brother James, who was four years older, entered the profession after graduating from Creighton University Medical School (getting married on the same day) in 1951; while the oldest brother, Jasper, who had previously earned a degree in business administration and accounting, went back to college and became a doctor in 1953. All of them interned at Provident Hospital . . . one of the few hospitals in the United States that would at that time accept blacks.

Each of them served in the Army during the Second World War, and all left the service as first lieutenants. When Mr. Williams received a letter saying that Jasper was in New York "fixing" to go to Europe to fight in the war he collapsed with a stroke on the street and had to be taken to the hospital. From that

227

point on he was never able to work again. Whether the stroke resulted from a sense of resentment that a government he had been suing for the past quarter-century—over his dismissal for refusing to clean out a cuspidor when he had been hired by the U.S. Department of Customs as a mail carrier and not a janitor —was now taking his son, or whether it was simply an overwhelming anxiety that his eldest might be killed will never be known.

The dynasty in the early fifties was beginning to take form, and Clara, retiring from teaching after fifty years, left Las Cruces for Omaha to help attend to Jasper's two young children, Carolyn and Jasper, Jr., while he was completing his last year in medical school. The three brothers admit that it is their mother who is the glue that binds the family together. "Whenever someone gets a big head, Grandma puts him in his place," admits Dr. Jasper Williams, Jr. Because each specialized in a different field, the idea occurred to them in the early sixties to pool their talent and form a clinic in the black section of Chicago known as Woodlawn. Clara Williams invested her life savings. Others were not so quick to step forward as the three brothers were turned down by several "white banks," and it was not until a black dermatologist by the unlikely name of Dr. T. K. Lawless cosigned a note for $150,000 with the Service Federal Savings and Loan Association that the clinic became a reality. Mrs. James Williams, who helps manage the clinic (virtually the whole family performs some function in the clinic; Mrs. James Williams' mother attends the switchboard; Clara worked there as a receptionist until she was ninety), remembers that one of her first management functions was to devise a method of paging doctors so that when "Calling Dr. Williams" came over the intercom, three, then five, and soon to be seven, Williamses would not appear all at once. She devised a method of simply calling them by their first name which while creating a pleasant air of informality, also makes it from time to time sound like the court of the Stuart kings gone bonkers. "James the first, report to surgery . . . Charles the first, report to dentistry . . . Charles the second, report to obstetrics . . . James the second, report," etc., etc., etc. But the person who has expressed Clara best is her granddaughter, Brenda, a reporter on the *Oakland Tribune* in California who wrote on her grandmother's ninety-fifty birthday:

"Thank you for the invaluable lessons, the subtle and unobtrusive ways you have shown me how to live long and decently and usefully. You have shown me how to offer the world the positive lessons you have learned and how to forget the negative ones that taught nothing. How not to get excited (in your words). How to be kind and wise and generous. How to be simple and good and honest. How to fight for what is right and how to survive when you lose. How to be strong and smart and sharp.

"How a woman can live alone in the world. How to have people remember you and love you after forty years. How to stay trim and handsome. How to roll your hair. How to be understanding and tolerant. How to love and how to let people know you love them. How to look up a word in the dictionary. How to love your children and grandchildren and great-grandchildren differently and equally.

"How to understand what people need. How to make plants grow. How to be independent. How to build a family and an institution and how to hold them together. How to overlook people's failings and forgive their meanness. How to save money. How to be agile and quick at ninety-five. How to be down-to-earth and concerned about the future of black people. How to be polite. And optimistic. How to see the statuesque beauty of a woman with an afro. How to adapt to a century's worth of changes. How to live more than one hundred years.

"With deepest love, respect, and gratitude, Brenda."

"Let me show you this picture," commands Grandma, taking my wrist. "These are my great-grandchildren Melody Clare and Nicole Allegro. Melody is a musical term as is Allegro, and I gave

229

their mother Carolyn, who teaches music, a baby grand piano so that my great-grandchildren could take music. They're taking music now . . . I see to that. I will help her find a direction." Clara Williams has helped two generations of her family find their direction and there is no reason to believe, "God willing" as she says, that she won't be successful in doing the same for the third. She is not the mother of the year. She is Big Mama of the century.

CLARABELLE WILLIAMS

1885 Born Clarabelle Drisdale, La Grange, Texas

1901 Received four-year scholarship award to the Prairie State Normal and Industrial College

1905 Valedictorian of her class; taught at Cameron, Texas

1907 Met Jasper Williams

1912 Attended summer school in Chicago

1917 Married Jasper Williams and moved to El Paso

1918 Sons Jasper born

1918 Purchased the Williams Drugstore

1919 Son James born

1923 Son Charles born

1924 Williams Drugstore burned to the ground
Taught school at Las Cruces

1928 Jasper Williams purchased homestead

1937 Clarabelle became first black to graduate from the New Mexico College of Agriculture and Mechanical Arts

1946 Jasper Williams died

1946–1953 Charles, James, Jasper received M.D. degrees

1960 Williams Clinic in Woodlawn section of Chicago established by the brothers

1966 Clara received Outstanding Mother and Businesswoman award by the Fine Arts Guild in Chicago

1977 Awarded Scroll of Merit from National Medical Association and elected to the National Education Association's Hall of Fame

1980 Honorary LL.D., University of Mexico

Clarabelle and family

Wedding pictures, 1917

Jasper Jr., Jasper Sr., James Sr., Charles Jr., Charles Sr.

Awarded honorary degree from New Mexico State University in 1980; (left to right) James Sr., Charles Sr., Jasper Sr.

Clarabelle today

Rosalyn S. Yalow

"PEOPLE TEND TO CONFUSE NUCLEAR MEDICINE WITH NUCLEAR REACTORS AND NUCLEAR BOMBS"

October 13, 1977. Special to *The New York Times:* "Three Americans, including a woman from the Bronx, were awarded the Nobel Prize in Physiology of Medicine today for their pioneering research into the role of hormones in the chemistry of the human body."

Of all the honors we have devised to recognize either a person's contribution to mankind or to promote a cause, it seems safe to say that none carries more distinction than the Nobel Prize. It has been given almost exclusively to men, particularly in the field of medicine, where only two women have been its recipients. As to the entire science category only six women have been so honored since Alfred Bernhard Nobel—the inventor of dynamite—set up under his will a trust to finance the honorarium back in 1896.

Rosalyn S. Yalow, too, would have undoubtedly forgone this honor if she had taken the advice of her parents and become an elementary schoolteacher because "it seemed unlikely that any good graduate schools in physics would accept and offer financial support for a woman." Fortunately, her physics professors were

235

Linda Hackett

of a dissenting opinion and convinced the then Rosalyn Sussman, whose academic record showed a pioneer overachiever, to remain with science. Along with her outstanding scholastic ability, Rosalyn must have also been blessed with a strong sense of self-reliance, for years later she was to write, "A child must learn from the cradle that upward mobility depends upon what people themselves do."

Her father, Simon Sussman, had only an eighth-grade education and worked as a jobber selling paper and twine while her mother, in order to supplement the family's income, took in sewing from an uncle's neckware factory. In the afternoons after school Rosalyn would help her by turning collars before she did her homework. Even though neither of Rosalyn's parents had received an education beyond that of eighth grade, they were determined that she and her brother would go to college. As a student in what was known as the rapid advancement class at P.S. 10, where the seventh, eighth, and ninth grades were completed in two years, Rosalyn needed time to study, but not as much as most. But she maintains, "I was not different from my friends. The neighborhood challenge was to see who would be the first to get into the library when it opened so there was nothing special about my family. . . . The Jews are known as people of the book, that is to say people of the Bible, but reading goes beyond the Bible, and ours is a culture in which learning is always important. Whether or not you migrate, you take your cultural heritage with you and ours goes back thousands of years."

When Yalow speaks there are no hesitations. The sentences spoken with a slightly nasal, slightly Bronx accent, come out in a smooth stream, and when she makes her point a smile that starts in her eyes radiates across her face like a sunrise spreading over the landscape. Yet looking at her you can believe her mother's claim that she was a "stubborn, determined child and it was fortunate that she chose to do acceptable things for if she had chosen otherwise, no one could have deflected her from her path." The acceptable things that Rosalyn chose were first mathematics and then chemistry at Walton High School in the Bronx. Here both the head of the Mathematics Department and a chemistry teacher took a special interest in what they must have recognized as a particularly gifted child. "People used to say that I made a good role model for women in science, whereas in fact all the teachers who influenced me were men."

At Hunter College for Women in New York City, she became interested in physics. When her family wanted her to become an elementary schoolteacher, it was Professor Jerrold Zacharias at Hunter College who persuaded her to continue in physics and got her a job as secretary to a leading biochemist of the day, Dr. Rudolph Schoenheimer, at the College of Physicians and Surgeons in Manhattan. In 1945, Dr. Maurice Goldhaber, who later became Director of Brookhaven National Laboratories, was the perceptor for her Ph.D. in nuclear physics. Two years later it was Dr. G. Failla, the Dean of American Medical Physicists, who recommended her for the staff of the Veterans' Administration Hospital in the Bronx. Two years after that Dr. Solomon A. Berson joined her and together they began a twenty-two-year collaboration which led to the development of radioimmunoassay (RIA) and earned for Dr. Yalow the Nobel Prize. Dr. Berson would have shared the prize had he not died in 1972—five years before this honor was awarded.

While it is true that it has been the "men in her life" who have been her influence and her inspiration, Rosalyn Yalow is also aware of the discrimination she faced in the early years of her career. "When I was admitted to the University of Illinois, in 1941, I was the first woman to receive a graduate assistanceship in physics since 1917. Well, everybody knows what 1941 and 1917 had in common—they both had the draft—and that is probably why Illinois accepted me. But things have improved since then. For example, up to about 1971 there was a decided quota against women in medical schools, and then things loosened up.

In 1971 only 11 percent of the graduating class in medical schools were women whereas the entering class that year had 22 percent, which meant that in a three-year period there was a doubling of the number of women entering medical school. However, I do not believe that this relaxation was so much due to the women's movement as to the Civil Rights movement which resulted in laws against discrimination."

While Dr. Yalow may abhor discrimination, she saves her real aversion for reverse discrimination. "I believe in equal opportunity . . . I do not believe in setting aside places for the previously disadvantaged. I resent there being special awards for women because it suggests tht women aren't competitive in the real world. I think that women who are competitive belong where the competition is, and they must demonstrate their capability in the real world."

If one thing marks Dr. Yalow's career, it is the fact that she has always been a fighter. As a junior at Hunter she remembers the competition to get into Pupin Laboratories at Columbia to hear Enrico Fermi give a colloquium in 1939 on the newly discovered nuclear fission. At the University of Illinois she was the only woman among the four hundred members on the faculty of the College of Engineering. She was equally competitive when she returned to New York in January 1945 to become the only woman engineer in the I.T.T. research laboratory. At graduate school she received all A's except in laboratory work for which she received an A—, which prompted the chairman of the Physics Department to comment that it just went to show that "women do not do well in laboratory work." It was on her first day at graduate school that she met Aaron Yalow, who was also working in physics. Apparently what struck him about Miss Sussman was not so much the fact that she was the only woman among four hundred men, but that her Bronx accent was difficult to ignore. He admits that as an upstate New Yorker, "I made some snide remarks about it." They were married two years later.

While the number of women who have earned Ph.D.'s in physics during the past half-century has remained at about a steady 2 percent of the total recipients, their psychological approach to marriage has, according to Yalow, changed. "Though the number of women in the field has remained constant, most of those who went on in science in 1921, when I was born, remained unmarried, whereas most of those that went on in science in 1971 were married. The feeling now seems to be that you can lead a normal life and still go into science. Contrary to the belief of women scientists in the twenties and thirties who held that women should not be married if they were to take on the hard life of science, I recognized early on that in order to be a good scientist, you really must have an integrated existence."

But she believes you also have to plan your life well, so she delayed having children for almost nine years until well established in her job as a physicist and assistant chief of the Radioisotope Service of the Veterans' Administration Hospital in the Bronx. In fact, she was so well established by then that she was allowed to remain at work up to the last minute and took off only a week each for the births of a son and a daughter. At that time government regulations required that women had to resign in their fifth month of pregnancy. "You didn't get maternity leave, you resigned." Yet Dr. Yalow was so important to the V.A. hospital that she did neither. Let the record show that she is the only women to have had, not one, but two 8-pound 2-ounce babies born in their fifth month. Dr. Yalow's husband, Aaron, is a professor of physics at Cooper Union and "enormously supportive of me and my work. You must choose a husband in keeping with the life-style that you want" is her advice to young lovers.

The life work that Rosalyn Yalow has chosen for herself is based on what Robert Oppenheimer has characterized as the "growing bud" of civilization. In her case the bud was nourished on the basic research which produced a whole new technology. Her work has to do with nuclear medicine and the development of a system of measuring the concentrations of "virtually any substance of biologic interest in the fluids and tissues of the body." One of many results of this research is a standard test used to determine whether the thyroid is underactive in the newly born, a condition that, if left untreated, will doom the child to mental retardation. "Previously an underactive thyroid could not be detected until the baby was several months old and by that time it was too late because adequate amounts of the thyroid hormone are crucial for normal brain development during the first few months of life. However, just a few drops of the neonate's blood can now be sent to a state or regional laboratory in most parts of the country at a cost of about a dollar or two per sample, and diagnosis can be made using RIA methodology within a week or two. The necessary treatment consisting of a small pill crushed in the infant's milk can begin promptly. It is now known that children so treated can grow up with a normal intellectual development. Using the same procedure, tests can also be made to determine whether the small stature of some children is due to the failure to properly produce or secrete growth hormone or to test for overactivity of the parathyroid gland which often leads to kidney stones.

The process developed by Dr. Yalow and her colleague is known as radioimmunoassay (RIA). It involves the application of nuclear physics to medicine using radioactive isotopes as a means of measuring against a known standard the concentration of hundreds of substances such as drugs, hormone viruses, vitamins, etc., contained in the blood and other biologic fluids of the human body. In addition to measuring hormone secretion it can be used to screen blood in blood banks for possible virus contamination which is responsible for producing hepatitis in transfused patients. RIA is employed to determine the degree of protection that an antirabies injection affords the victims of a dog bite; it can serve to determine whether drugs and antibiotics prescribed for treatment measure up to the required dosage and, conversely, it

can be used to determine whether an overdose of heroin, metho-
done, LSD, or other drugs have been taken or surreptitiously
administered.

But because RIA employs radioactive material, there is controversy about the disposal of accompanying wastes. "This has been
a major fight of mine over the past year and a half," Dr. Yalow says.
"There is so much misunderstanding on the whole subject."
Anthropologists maintain that during the early periods of development, men had words for bison, reindeer, and mammoth, but
lacked the symbols for broader categories, such as the term ani-
mal. We have, Dr. Yalow explains, the reverse situation in that we
can discuss the abstract atom but can't differentiate between the
different nuclear animals. The nuclear animals, according to Dr.
Yalow, are three: nuclear medicine, nuclear reactors, and nuclear
bombs; each serves a different purpose and one should not be
confused with the other. "People tend to confuse nuclear medicine with nuclear reactors and nuclear bombs . . . they just hear the
world nuclear and make no distinction as to its application. I have
calculated that the amounts of radioactive carbon and radioactive
hydrogen involved that are disposed of in New York State are less
than one percent of the radioactive carbon released by our garbage or one percent of the radioactive hydrogen in rainfall on the
city of New York. We have a pathological fear of radiation, and it is
interfering with the job of getting on with the business of doing
biomedical investigation, which really saves lives."

Whenever the subject of the disposition of nuclear wastes
arises, the inevitable question surfaces about nuclear power
plants and their potential hazard. Dr. Yalow is not reticent about
voicing her opinion on this subject. The radiation coming from
a nuclear plant is less than the amount of radiation coming from
a coal plant. "I wish our country would go the way of being
self-sufficient in energy, which it could with nuclear power. Nuclear war is more of a threat because of our dependence on
foreign oil. If we were self-sufficient and the Russians were self-

sufficient and other smaller countries were self-sufficient in terms of energy—and this is possible with nuclear power—then there would be fewer reasons for fighting. No, I think nuclear power will prevent war, not foment it."

Dr. Yalow's tiny office, way in the back of one of the wings of the old V.A. building in the Bronx, looks like a hangout for one of the Collier brothers, so packed is it with books and pamphlets, clippings, and scientific papers. Columns of books sit on the floor, sheaves of papers blanket her desk, scientific journals and clippings sprout from nooks and crannies like straw from a scarecrow. If not all, at least most of the information contained within them has convinced her that the prudent way to go is nuclear and the reason we are not proceeding in this direction may be a well-orchestrated conspiracy to denigrate atomic energy. "You know," she says, going on to explain her position, "the best-kept secret in America is the fact that any harmful effect due to the release of radioactive material from a melt-down of an atomic reactor has about the same probability as that Skylab would have fallen on New York City. If there had been a complete melt-down at Three Mile Island nobody would have been hurt. Now this information never gets to the public; it gets only to the scientists. The public only gets the nonsense." She believes that this information which is well known to the scientific community is being hushed up for some "diabolical reason."

In years past when Dr. Yalow was asked to speak before a group she would always refuse unless her audience was doctors or scientists, but now because of her belief that the American public is almost totally misinformed with regard to the potential and risks of nuclear energy, she speaks more frequently at university campuses and public meetings. She admits that before she received the Nobel Prize she was, like most scientists, happy to "hide in her laboratory and not face the real world." That is no longer true, so, real world, brace yourself, for Rosalyn S. Yalow is beginning to react.

ROSALYN
S. YALOW

Yalow in her laboratory

1921   Born Rosalyn Sussman, New York

1941   A.B., Hunter College, physics and chemistry

1941–1943   Assistant in Physics, University of Illinois

1942   M.S., University of Illinois, physics

1943   Married Aaron Yalow

1944–1945   Instructor, University of Illinois

1945   Ph.D., University of Illinois, physics

1946–1950   Lecturer and Temporary Assistant Professor, Physics, Hunter College

1947–1950   Consultant, Radioisotope Unit, Veterans' Administration Hospital, The Bronx, New York

1952   Son Benjamin born

1952–1962   Consultant, Lenox Hill Hospital

1950–1970   Physicist and Assistant Chief, Radioisotope Service, V.A. Hospital

1954   Daughter Elanna born

1968–1970   Acting Chief, Radioisotope Service, V.A. Hospital

1968–1974   Research Professor, Department of Medicine, Mt. Sinai School of Medicine

1969   Chief, V.A. Radioimmunoassay Reference Laboratory

1970–1980   Chief, Nuclear Medicine Service, V.A. Hospital

1974–1979   Distinguished Service Professor, Mt. Sinai School of Medicine

Yalow, her mother Clara Sussman (96), and her daughter Elanna (27)

*Receiving Nobel Prize from King
Gustaf*

Aaren and Rosalyn on their home computer

Nobel Prize medals

1977	Nobel Prize in Physiology Medicine
1979–Present	Distinguished Professor-at-Large, Albert Einstein College of Medicine, Yeshiva University, New York
1980–Present	Chairman, Department of Clinical Sciences, Montefiore Hospital and Medical Center, The Bronx, New York

PICTURE CREDITS

Abbott
Man Ray, courtesy *Vanity Fair*. © 1922, Renewed 1960 by The Condé Nast Publications Inc.
James Joyce, courtesy *Vanity Fair*. © 1933, renewed 1961 by The Condé Nast Publications Inc.
Park Row, courtesy International Center of Photography
Andre Kertesz and Abbott by John Abrams, courtesy International Center of Photography
Rita Hillman, William Lieberman, Bernice Abbott and Cornell Capa, by John Abrams, courtesy International Center of Photography
Lecturing, by John Abrams, courtesy International Center of Photography

Belcher
Crawford in ambulance, courtesy Dr. Belcher
Four generations, courtesy Dr. Belcher
Waiting room, by Linda Hackett
Examination room, by Linda Hackett
Belcher 1983, by Linda Hackett

Benet
All photos courtesy Dr. Benet, except Benet in office, by Bill Cunningham

Blackwell
Mademoiselle covers, courtesy *Mademoiselle*

Brown
Young Mrs. Brown, courtesy Mrs. Brown
Mrs. Brown's house, by Nyholm, courtesy *Vogue*. © 1944, renewed 1972 by The Condé Nast Publications Inc.
Eleanor and Archibald Brown, by E. F. Foley, courtesy Mrs. Brown
Living room, by Nyholm, courtesy *Vogue*. © 1944, renewed 1972 by The Condé Nast Publications Inc.
Rosedown, by Tom Leonard, courtesy *House and Garden*. © 1964 by The Condé Nast Publications Inc.
Brown and Walter Hoving, by Jeanne Trudeau. © 1982, courtesy McMillen Inc.

Bunting
Walking in Wisconsin, courtesy Dr. Bunting
Bunting with her children, courtesy Radcliffe College Archives
Bunting, Harvard Seminar, courtesy Dr. Bunting
Bunting and baby, courtesy Dr. Bunting
Bunting and Mary, by Ester Bubley, courtesy *Life*
Aerial view of Radcliffe, courtesy Radcliffe College Archives
Radcliffe pamphlets, courtesy Radcliffe College Archives

Radcliffe demonstration, courtesy Dr. Bunting
Bunting, © 1972, Josef Karsk; courtesy Dr. Bunting

Frissell
Courtesy *Vogue*. © 1941 by the Condé Nast Publications Inc.
London, courtesy Frissell Collection, Library of Congress
Fashion shot, courtesy *Vogue*
Bacon's house, photo by George Hoitis, courtesy *Vogue*. © 1973 by The Condé Nast Publications Inc.
Hallmark show, photo by Sack Anderson, courtesy Frissell Collection, Library of Congress
Hanging flowers, by George Hoitis, courtesy *Vogue*. © 1973 by The Condé Nast Publications Inc.

Harrison-Ross
All photos, courtesy Harrison-Ross, except
Family portrait, by Linda Hackett

Johnson and Masters
All photos, courtesy of Johnson, except impact chart, courtesy *Science Digest*

Leichter
Vienna, courtesy The Bettmann Archive
The Statue of Liberty, courtesy The Bettmann Archive
Leichter and friends, courtesy Mrs. Leichter
Johann S. Bach, courtesy The Bettmann Archive
Leichter today, by Bill Cunningham

McIntosh
Varsity captain, courtesy Barnard College Archives
Seven sister presidents, courtesy Barnard College Archives and the Poughkeepsie *New Yorker*
Breaking ground, courtesy Barnard College Archives
Commencement, by J. Hitchell, courtesy Barnard College Archives
Drs. McIntosh, courtesy Mrs. McIntosh

McWhinney
McWhinney and Smedley, courtesy *The New York Times*
McWhinney as president of First Woman's Bank, courtesy *Associated Press*
Promotional poster, courtesy *Wirephoto*
Gambling experts, courtesy *Asbury Park Press*

Motley
Motley, by Cecily Beaton, courtesy *Vogue*. © 1967 by The Condé Nast Publications Inc.
Martin Luther King, courtesy The Bettmann Archives
Foley Square, courtesy The Bettmann Archives
Motley in her chambers, by Linda Hackett

Parsons
Parsons at five, courtesy B. Parsons
Parsons as a young woman, courtesy B. Parsons
Steinberg's portrait of Parsons, courtesy Geoffery Clements
Parsons, by Pousette-Dart
Southold, by Naar, courtesy *House and Garden.* © 1967 by The Condé
   Nast Publications Inc.
Parsons with dog, courtesy B. Parsons

Porter
Aline in study, living room, and Eliot in studio, by Ernst Beadle, courtesy
   House and Garden. © 1977 by The Condé Nast Publications, Inc.
Piece, courtesy Betty Parsons Gallery

Rosenberg
With General Patten, courtesy Mr. Rosenberg
With American troops, courtesy Mr. Rosenberg
Receiving Medal of Honor, by U.S. Army Signal Corps
With General Jenkins, by *Associated Press*
In Korea, by Sargeant G. Kelemanik, courtesy U.S. Army photography

Vreeland
In Arizona, by Louise Dahl-Wolfe, courtesy D. Vreeland
Vreeland, by Christian Bayard, courtesy D. Vreeland
Costumes, by Duane Michals, courtesy *Vogue.* © 1979 by The Condé
   Nast Publications Inc.
In front of portrait. © 1979, by Jonathan Becker

Williams
Wedding pictures, reprinted by permission, *Ebony Magazine,* © 1980, by
   Johnson Publishing Co., Inc.
The Doctors, reprinted by permission from *Ebony Magazine,* © 1980, by
   Johnson Publishing Co., Inc.
Family, courtesy Mrs. Williams
Awarded degree, reprinted by permission from *Ebony Magazine,* © 1980,
   by Johnson Publishing Co., Inc.
Clarabelle today, photo by Austad, courtesy Chicago *Tribune*

Yalow
In her laboratory, courtesy the Medical Media Department, V.A. Medical
   Center, Bronx
With King Gustaf of Sweden, courtesy *Reportagebild*
Aaron and Roslyn, by Georgiana Silk
With mother and daughter, by Georgiana Silk
Nobel Prize, courtesy the Medical Media Department, V.A. Medical Cen-
   ter, Bronx